D1715437

The Salem Witch Hunt

A Captivating Guide to the Hunt and Trials of People Accused of Witchcraft in Colonial Massachusetts

Had charity been put on, the Devil would not have had such an advantage against us.

- Rev. Francis Dane

Free Bonus from Captivating History (Available for a Limited time)

Hi History Lovers!

Now you have a chance to join our exclusive history list so you can get your first history ebook for free as well as discounts and a potential to get more history books for free! Simply visit the link below to join.

Captivatinghistory.com/ebook

Also, make sure to follow us on Facebook, Twitter and Youtube by searching for Captivating History.

Contents

Introduction

The name Salem has become synonymous for witchcraft. Despite the fact that the town, now known as Danvers, Massachusetts, has been standing for close to 400 years, a little more than 12 months of its history has become the town's very definition: the Salem witch hunt.

Decades after witch-hunting had begun to die down in Europe, North America was about to witness its bloodiest witch hunt in history. The Massachusetts of 1692 was a very different one to the state we know today. Populated by colonists, many of them a generation or less from life in an England bathed in religious turmoil, Massachusetts was not the safe haven that the fleeing Puritans had hoped it would be. Persecuted for their faith in Europe, the Puritans had pictured a kind of utopia founded on biblical principles. They saw the New World as a new beginning, a kind of second chance for humanity. It would be only 72 years after the arrival of the *Mayflower* that the events in Salem would make it blatantly obvious that humanity had already blown it again.

It is still not quite clear why exactly the witch hunt began in the first place or what caused the symptoms of those who had been said to be afflicted by witchcraft. It may have been a conspiracy by a group of the villagers, a bid for attention by girls who were repressed by their families and society, or even the result of poisoning by a fungus that grows on rye bread. The result, however, was the same: more than twenty people were killed, most of them by hanging, some dying in the awful conditions of 17th-century Bostonian jails, and one crushed to death in a horrendous act of torture.

Yet this is not the story of the trials. This is the story of its people. This is not an attempt to explain the events of 1692. It is an attempt to bring to life the victims who died so unjustly. In this book, we will walk side by side with the destitute Sarah Good as she realizes that after having lost all she owns, her reputation, her baby, and even her life will still be taken from her. We stand at the bar with Rebecca Nurse, a sweet little old lady who is sentenced to hang for what she must have perceived to be the most heinous of crimes. We witness George Burroughs at the gallows, a former minister now condemned to die for his supposed alliance with Satan, as he delivers a speech so stirring that it takes quick thinking from his enemies to prevent the crowd from rushing forth to cut him down. We feel our own breaths catching as we watch the cruel and greedy Sheriff George Corwin piling rocks onto the fragile eighty-year-old body of Giles Corey, who is determined to die without entering a plea so that his sons will still get the inheritance he promised them.

We will walk through this history in the footprints of those who suffered the hardest in it. The Salem witch hunt and trials killed many and ruined the lives of countless others. And this is their story.

Prologue – The Hanging of Goody Glover

The old lady had shifting eyes that darted from face to face in the noisome crowd. They were yelling at her, mocking her, flinging slurs at her like fistfuls of mud. In sharp contrast to Boston's fall colors that blazed all around her, the old woman seemed colorless, wrung out, like a ragged piece of clothing that had been through the laundry one time too many. She muttered constantly as they led her up the hill among the brightly colored trees, and onlookers whispered among themselves. "It's the devil's language," some said. "It's gibberish—she's mad," said others. And a tiny portion, those who—like the old woman—had been uprooted from their native Ireland due to events entirely out of their control, recognized that the language was neither of hell nor of insanity. It was just Gaelic: the frightened, mumbled Gaelic of an Irishwoman condemned to die.

The gallows were waiting. They cast a thin shadow over the crowd, a black and angular shape, cold and sharp in the balmy November day. The noose swung gently in the breeze as the old lady clambered up to the platform.

Among the crowd was a Bostonian merchant by the name of Robert Calef, and he watched with sorrow and horror as the noose was arranged around the old lady's neck. He'd known her for some time, and to his mind, Ann "Goody" Glover was nothing but a fragile old lady—a little crazy, perhaps, and a bit of an outsider, but there was nothing threatening about her. Still, it was not for him to go against what the colonial government of Massachusetts had decided.

There was a yelp of panic from the crowd. Robert spun around and spotted a pitiful sight: Goody Glover's cat meowing in distress as it was snatched up by the scruff of its neck. The crowd shrieked for its neck to be wrung, panicking. Was this a demon? Some kind of a familiar? They didn't want to know—they just wanted it dead. Robert couldn't let this happen, too. He pushed the crowd aside, his burly form shouldering them out of the way, and snatched the cat out of its aggressor's hands. Shouting that it was just an innocent animal, Robert cradled the little creature to his chest. Wisely, the crowd decided against pushing the issue.

Goody herself was not so easy to save. In fact, the resigned look in her eyes made it seem as though she, too, knew she was past saving. She only had one thing left to say. As they were making the preparations to hang her, she spoke up in Gaelic. Some of the crowd shied back, panicking, but those among them who understood her knew what she was saying. It wasn't a threat. It was a simple, resigned statement: "My death will not save those children from their malady." It's unclear exactly why she said that, but it mattered little to those present. They dropped the trapdoor anyway.

She fell but only a few inches. The rope yanked tight. Her feet swung and kicked on the end of arthritic old knees but found no purchase. She choked once, and then she died: the last witch of Boston.

Chapter 1 – Witches in Europe

Illustration I: An 1853 painting by Tompkins Harrison Matteson entitled Examination of a Witch

https://commons.wikimedia.org/wiki/File:Examination_of_a_Witch_-_Tompkins_Matteson.jpg

Goody Glover was hanged on November 16th, 1688, after charges of witchcraft were laid against her and she was found guilty by the government of Massachusetts Bay Colony. Born in Ireland, she was forced out of her home country by the 1649 to 1653 invasion of Oliver Cromwell, from whence she was likely shipped to Barbados as an indentured servant. By the time she died in North America, she hadn't seen her home country for 35 years.

Goody had tried to make the best of her new life in the New World. She was married when in Barbados and had a young daughter by the name of Mary, and while work on the sugar plantation wasn't easy, at least she had a family and a place to call—more or less—home. The Glover family was not exactly accepted in their new home, though. As the wars of religion had been ravaging Europe for decades, many Puritans and Protestants saw the New World as a way to escape the tyrannical fist of the Roman Catholic Church, and the Glover family's Irish Catholicism was greatly unwelcome. Allegedly, it was so unwelcome that Mr. Glover was executed for his faith.

Goody and Mary ended up being sent north to work in one of the English colonies, setting up in Boston as housekeepers for one John Goodwin. Impoverished, but at least now considered to be free, Goody and Mary were trying to carve out an existence for themselves. Perhaps their need was too great for Mary to bear; at any rate, in 1688, John Goodwin's teenage daughter Martha accused Mary of stealing some clothes when she and her mother were doing laundry. A fight ensued between Goody and the Goodwin children, but things seemed to be ironed out fairly quickly, and everyone went back to work or play.

That was until the Goodwin children suddenly fell horribly, terrifyingly ill. They were seized by terrible spasms that wracked their young bodies, making them scream in pain; night terrors gripped them, leaving them yelling about the horrible things that they were seeing and hearing. Some accounts had them trying to fly like geese or barking like dogs at one another. John Goodwin's children had all gone suddenly and inexplicably mad. Or perhaps not so inexplicably, according to their physician. He could find nothing physically wrong with them, he said. The only explanation for their behavior was witchcraft.

And when authorities discovered Goody Glover muttering in "Satan's language" and stumbled upon crudely made dolls in her home, and when religious writer Cotton Mather's translator said that Goody had told him she worshiped "spirits," it seemed that Boston had found its witch. It mattered little that Goody spoke a broken mixture of English and Gaelic when she was panicked or that, as a Catholic, she prayed to images of saints—likely the "spirits" that she had told Mather about. The government's mind was made up. Goody Glover was a witch, and she would hang.

Hang she did, but her chilling last words did come true: those children didn't get better until 1689, even under Mather's close ministrations. Some said that she had made the prediction because she'd been working with other witches. Others said that she'd spoken as an innocent woman. Either way, Goody was dead. And while she marked the last witch to be hanged in Boston itself, she would not be the last person in Massachusetts to die.

The madness was just beginning.

* * * *

The Puritans that condemned Goody Glover to die, officially because she was a witch but more likely simply due to the fact that she was Catholic, would have been horrified to find out that the very act of executing a witch was a very Catholic invention. In fact, it was a papal bull issued by Pope Innocent VIII that made the condemnation of witchcraft official in 1484—almost a decade before Columbus ever set sight on the New World. The bull spurred two of the Church's Inquisitors to write *The Hammer of Witches*, a book detailing how witches were evil and giving thorough instructions on how to identify and then destroy them. Worst of all, the book did not require any form of fair, legal evidence to justify the killing or execution of a witch. It started an age in which superstition was grounds for taking a human life.

The publication of *The Hammer of Witches* spurred on a witch-hunting mania that quickly spread throughout all of Europe. At that time, the continent was under a lot of pressure from the Roman Catholic Church, which was more powerful than most kingdoms or countries. When a papal bull was issued, it went everywhere, and when two members of the terrifying Inquisition published a book, it was taken seriously.

Witchcraft had been condemned as evil for thousands of years by this point, starting with the Hebrew scriptures of old. It was only after Pope Innocent's decree, however, that the real witch-hunting madness began. While "white magic" had been a tradition in England for centuries—probably a leftover of the ancient mythologies that had been in place there before it was conquered in 1066—there was a clear distinction between these small superstitions and what was considered to be witchcraft. Witchcraft was thought of as "black magic": a literal deal with the devil, trading one's soul in loyalty to him in exchange for all kinds of supernatural powers.

In only a few decades, spates of witch-hunting broke loose throughout Europe, most notably in the Holy Roman Empire. Witches were blamed for almost everything: bad weather, infertility, illness, plagues of pests, even the deaths of people or livestock. By the start of the 16th century, Germany was engaged in a fervent witch hunt that claimed hundreds of lives. Witchcraft was made a secular crime in countries as technologically advanced as England and Russia, and witches were burned at the stake in terrifying numbers, executed on the basis of little more than rumors and coincidences.

Even as the balance of power changed throughout the world, with the rise of Protestantism shaking the foundations of the Christian faith as Catholicism started to lose some of its power, the hunting of witches continued. In fact, witch-hunting reached its highpoint early in the 17th century, over 120 years after the publication of *The Hammer of Witches*.

It was in 1612 that the Pendle witch trials occurred. Despite the fact that England only saw about 500 people executed for witchcraft during the entire period of the witch-hunting craze—compared to an estimate of around 40,000 people killed throughout Europe—the most notorious of all the witch trials took place in Lancashire. And while they involved fewer people than their American cousins would eighty years later, the Pendle witch trials set the precedents that made the Salem trials so deadly.

* * * *

Jennet Device should never have testified. In fact, her name should have never even been written down; she should have been utterly lost in the fog of history, a little life blowing by as temporary as a dandelion seed in the wind. She was just a beggar, an illegitimate girl living in the harsh reality of early 17th-century England—an era ruled over by the zealous King James I. She was nobody. Worst of all, she was a nobody from Lancashire, a particularly troublesome part of the kingdom. The residents of Lancashire were devoted Catholics, despite the Crown's loyalty to the Anglican Church, and they had been a thorn in James' side ever since he ascended to the throne of England in 1603.

Roger Nowell, the new Justice of the Peace stationed in Lancaster Castle, was determined to change that. He would whip those Catholics right into form, earning a sizable feather in his cap from King James while he was about it. And it was Alizon Device, a beggar from the village of Pendle, who would provide him with the perfect opportunity.

Alizon was begging her way along the road past Trawden Forest when she came across a peddler by the name of John Law. Seeing the dodgy-looking beggar woman coming at him, Law did his best to avoid her, but she was persistent. She came up to him—a foul, unwashed creature, even by the unhygienic standards of the era—and demanded of him to give her some pins (pins were frequently used for magical purposes, such as for treating warts or for love magic). Repulsed, Law strongly refused, and Alizon responded by cursing him in a way that made all his hair stand on end. He escaped unscathed, or at least, so he thought. Shortly thereafter, Law was struck down by a debilitating stroke. The only logical explanation he could think of was that Alizon Device was a witch, and she had cursed him.

In the following few days, Justice Nowell would be delighted to discover what he believed to be an entire nest full of witches. When Alizon was questioned, not only did she confess to having cursed John Law, but she dragged the entire Chattox family into it as well. The Chattoxes had been enemies of Alizon's family for years, and since Alizon believed in her own powers and was certain she would be prosecuted for witchcraft, it only made sense to take her enemies down with her.

The Chattox family refused to confess, and that might have been the end of it if it hadn't been for nine-year-old Jennet Device. The sister of Alizon and the daughter of Elizabeth Device, who was also implicated as a witch, Jennet could not have had much of a childhood living with a beggar woman who was either fanatically convinced of her abilities to curse people—and willing to use those abilities for the smallest of transgressions—or was simply mentally ill. Whether Jennet was trying to get away from her crazy family or whether she was simply telling what a frightened child believed to be the truth is unclear. Either way, Jennet testified against her mother, brother, older sister, and grandmother, saying that they had held a gathering for witches and performed all kinds of dark magic. Ordinarily, anyone younger than fourteen would not have been accepted as a credible witness, but King James had ordered justices to discard all usual rules of evidence when it came to prosecuting witches. Jennet's testimony was all the condemnation that was necessary, even though she was just a scared little girl.

Gleefully, Justice Nowell arrested twelve people for witchcraft, including the Chattoxes and Jennet's entire family. Jennet's grandmother, Old Demdike, did not make it to the trial. She died in the festering dungeon of Lancaster Castle. Of the other eleven, only one —Alice Grey—was found not guilty. The remaining ten people, including Jennet's entire family, were found guilty and were condemned to death by hanging.

The Pendle witch trials have since been seen as a tragedy, with various statues and events celebrating their 400th anniversary in 2012. Eighty years after the Pendle trials took place, however, they would be horribly eclipsed by something far worse.

* * * *

Jennet Device was not safe from future witch hunts, however. Thirty years after her family was hanged based on her testimony, she found herself confronting her own accuser in court. This time, it was a boy: Edmund Robinson, only ten years old. He claimed that Jennet and sixteen of her acquaintances had performed witchcraft.

If James had still been on the throne, Jennet would likely have suffered the same fate as her family. But things had changed throughout England and Europe since the zealous king had died in 1625. Evidence had to be concrete, for one thing; no one could be hanged based simply on the testimony of a scared little kid. Jennet's trial dragged on for some time before Edmund finally admitted that he'd made the whole thing up. She was acquitted but probably lived out her life in captivity, unable to pay back the lodging that she owed the government after being in prison for some time.

Similar events were taking place across Europe. Instead of simply executing witches willy-nilly all over the continent, judges were starting to come down harder on accusers, demanding more solid evidence. By 1682, the King of France, Louis XIV, had banned witch trials in his country. That same year, England hanged its last two witches; by 1717, witch trials had formally ended in England, too. Austria, Hungary, and most of the other European countries would soon follow.

The madness that had gripped Europe for more than 200 years was finally coming to an end, but for colonial America, it had only just begun.

Chapter 2 – Salem

At the same time as people from all corners of Christianity were persecuting witches with considerable zeal, Christianity itself was profoundly divided.

During the Middle Ages, the Roman Catholic Church presided almost unopposed throughout Europe. Its popes enjoyed more power than most monarchs, standing on the same level as emperors. Almost every living person in the length and breadth of Europe was a practicing Catholic. Laws and methods of government were based almost entirely on the teachings of the Catholic Church, and actions that went against its doctrines—such as not partaking in Holy Communion—were crimes that could get you hanged or tortured.

All of this changed in the 16th century when theologian Martin Luther decided to stand against what he saw as the pomposity and ridiculous worldliness of the Catholic Church. He advocated for a simpler religion, one that he and many others saw as far more wholesome: they would still worship the same God, but they would strip away the ostentatious trappings of Catholicism. Luther's following turned into a wave of religious change throughout the continent that became known as Protestantism.

The Protestants had just started to make their voices heard in England when the English king, Henry VIII, demanded Pope Clement VII to annul his marriage to Catherine of Aragon. Catherine was forty years old and had failed to produce a male heir for Henry;

he saw no way out but to get rid of her. Considering that Catherine had family in high places—most notably the Holy Roman Emperor—the pope diplomatically declined. Infuriated, Henry broke his entire kingdom off from the Roman Catholic Church. Instead, he formed a new religious organization, the Church of England, placing himself at its head.

At once, some of the Protestants saw their chance. They wanted to reform the Church entirely, stripping away all of the elaborate rituals, props, and ceremonies of the Catholic Church. Others, however, were just happy to be rid of the pope and of the many monasteries that dotted the English landscape. The king was in favor of the latter sentiment; the Church of England that he designed was almost identical to the Catholic Church; it was still as pompous, and he essentially took on the role of the pope himself.

Those Protestants that demanded more dramatic reform soon became known as the Puritans. Their vociferous advocacy for a completely different Church, one based solely on Scripture and making no use of images or elaborate ceremonies, would eventually land them in trouble. When Charles I ascended to the throne in 1625, the Puritans saw their chance to make their voices heard against the Church of England and the king's role in it. Charles tried to solve this problem by not just by removing the Puritan members of Parliament but dissolving Parliament altogether. This last act left the Puritans frustrated and fed up. They decided that England itself was a lost cause and that the only way to have religious freedom was to build a whole new world.

Fortunately for them, a New World had recently been discovered.

* * * *

It is pretty ironic that the settlers who first arrived at Naumkeag decided to rename it "Salem," considering that the Hebrew word it is derived from—*Shalom*—means "peace."

The name, however, was more than a mere sentiment expressed by the Puritan people who had fled to the New World and settled in the area in an attempt to escape the relentless persecution that their religion had been suffering back home in Europe. In fact, it was renamed Salem because of an unusual occurrence for that era: a completely peaceful and diplomatic transition of leadership.

The story begins with Roger Conant. Conant was born in 1592 and grew up a Protestant in a time when England's religious conflicts were at their height. The Puritans foresaw trouble from King Charles even before he took the throne in 1625; in fact, in 1620, a group of Puritans known as the Pilgrims had departed England aboard the *Mayflower*, headed for the New World. They established the Plymouth Colony near Cape Cod, and three years later, Roger Conant would follow. He stayed in the Plymouth Colony for some time but was dissatisfied by what he saw there. Despite the Pilgrims' determination to build a new civilization of higher moral standards, Conant witnessed the cruel and harsh treatment of those who had committed dissent. The greatest culprit was Myles Standish, a captain in the military. Of him, Conant wrote that he "had forgotten his first lessons [in the church], to offer violence to no man." Unhappy with the new colony, in 1626, Conant decided to move his family farther north, to the mouth of the Naumkeag River. Some settlers joined him, and they established a small settlement named Naumkeag.

A few years later, in 1629, the Massachusetts Bay Colony realized that Naumkeag was struggling. The settlers that were trying, with such determination, to eke out a living from the rough new land were barely clinging on. Relief came in the form of John Endecott, the governor of the Massachusetts Bay Colony (and later the governor of the state of Massachusetts). Endecott brought with him the people and resources to build an entire town out of the settlement of Naumkeag, but he also brought a hot temper, strong convictions, and a determination to control everything. The settlers held their breath, expecting a fight to come out of it; Conant, they expected, would oppose Endecott by simply taking over everything he'd been struggling to build for the past three years. Instead, Conant peacefully handed over his role to Endecott. He was rewarded with some land and happily settled there, staying involved in the affairs of the town, but he was very much in Endecott's shadow.

The people were overjoyed and relieved that the transition had gone so well. They named their new settlement "Salem" after this unexpected peace and celebrated by continuing to thrive in the New World. In fact, it was in Salem that the first Puritan church in North America was built: the First Church of Salem. For a people that had been fleeing the harsh oppression of the Roman Catholic Church for decades, it was a welcome respite.

With Endecott and Conant working together to build the settlement into the town of Salem, the people soon began to thrive. By 1636, the first trade ship from Salem was headed out to the West Indies to sell salted cod. In 1644, Salem's first fort was built, showing how it had become established as a Massachusetts town. Other important buildings would follow: the Custom House, the House of the Seven Gables (featured in Nathaniel Hawthorne's novel of the same name; Hawthorne was born in Salem), and, pertinently, the Witch House.

Still standing today, the so-called Witch House was the home of Judge Jonathan Corwin. Corwin bought the house in 1675 as an affluent young man, looking to settle in a nice area with his family. Salem, by this point, was a bustling town, but it was by no means politically stable, mostly due to the chaos in the country where most of the settlers had come from, England.

Protestants were continuing to make waves in England and the rest of Europe, their movement growing in size until it was nothing short of intimidating. By 1688, their power had grown enough to orchestrate a revolution that deposed King James II and placed two Protestant rulers on the throne—the famed King William III and his wife, Queen Mary II. This caused considerable trouble for the colonies of the New World. Governors were replaced, and tensions wildly escalated between the colonists and the Wabanaki Confederacy. This Native American confederacy was backed by the might of France, which was a more stable country at the time than England, and the tension soon blew up into all-out war. Known as King William's War, it raged for nine years, making life even more difficult for the residents of Salem.

On a smaller scale, Salem was not at peace even with itself. The days of Conant and Endecott were long gone, taking the tolerance and diplomacy that had characterized their relationship with them. Now, Salem had split into two separate groups: Salem Town and Salem Village (present-day Danvers). Residents of Salem Village, in particular, were notorious for being difficult and argumentative. They refused to accept Salem Town's minister, instead finding their own, but their first two ministers quickly realized that the villagers were more trouble than they were worth. The second, George Burroughs, lasted only three years before resigning his post because he hadn't been paid. The third, Deodat Lawson, got along fine with the village but failed to be ordained by the parish and was more or less forced to resign in 1688.

* * * *

The villagers selected Samuel Parris to be Lawson's replacement, much to the chagrin of the parish. Perhaps the parish was right to be suspicious of him.

Parris had been born in London in 1653 and studied theology at Harvard as a young man. Before he could complete his courses, however, Parris' father died and left him with a sizable sugar plantation in Barbados. It would appear that Parris decided that the life of a church minister was not for him; he left London and Harvard behind in 1673, emigrating to Barbados and settling there. He leased out his plantation and also worked as a credit agent, helping other plantation owners to sell sugar. For seven years, he was a bustling businessman and seemed to be prospering. Then, in 1680, a devastating hurricane wiped out most of Parris' plantation. Dismayed, Parris had little choice but to walk away from his life again. He moved to Boston, taking his two slaves with him.

For a time, Parris seems to have been peacefully settled in Boston. He got married to Elizabeth Elridge and had three children with her, also establishing himself as a merchant, and the family was prospering when Parris decided once again that he wasn't content with his life. He wanted to return to his original occupation—that of a minister—and despite his lack of an official degree, he started speaking at gatherings and acting as a substitute for absent ministers.

The parish did not see Parris as very reliable, but Salem Village was adamant: they wanted him for their minister. Parris was not fazed by the fact that the villagers were reported to be obstinate and difficult. He moved his family—Elizabeth, their three children, his little niece Abigail, and the two slaves he'd brought from Barbados—into the parsonage of Salem Village. He was determined to whip those villagers into shape.

No matter the cost.

Chapter 3 – Strange Afflictions

Reverend Parris quickly learned just how difficult the congregation of Salem Village could be. Within a few months, he was up to his neck in arguing with them and not only over spiritual matters.

When Parris had first moved to Salem, he had been told that he would be given a small salary but also the ownership of the parsonage and its lands. The villagers would also provide him with firewood; someone would even go out and cut it for him. However, this did not last long. The villagers were soon saying that the parsonage was only his to use for the time that he was the minister of the village. The ugly disagreement ended up in court.

In the meantime, Parris cracked down hard on anyone who seemed to live in any way contrary to the teachings of his church. In fact, he made it compulsory for full members of the church to be baptized and to confess their faith publicly—a standard that was more lax in Salem Town and other Puritan colonies. While this made him very popular with those villagers who wore their status as full members of the church like badges of honor, others were not so enamored with his decision. It was likely these members who stirred up the trouble about the ownership of the parsonage in the first place.

The more trouble occurred, however, the harsher and stricter Parris became. He was a loud, overbearing man who tried to bully his congregation into obeying the strictest rules, and the harder the committee fought him, the more passive-aggressive he got, eventually starting to use his sermons to snap back at committee members by likening them to Satan. He was so badly liked that the villagers flatly refused to cut firewood for him or pay his salary anymore. It was only thanks to one dedicated family of supporters, the Putnams, that Parris and his family were kept afloat.

Little did Parris know that his troubles were only just beginning.

* * * *

Giggling, Abigail Williams and Elizabeth Parris gathered around the kitchen table. Betty's parents—Elizabeth and Samuel, the minister of the village—were conveniently absent. Elizabeth was likely lying in her sickbed as usual, and Samuel might have been off somewhere to preach or fight at a meeting. Abigail's parents were likely dead; she was a relative of the Parris family and lived in their house. The only people in the parsonage were Tituba and John Indian, the Parris family's Caribbean slaves. "Nabby" and "Betty" knew that neither of the slaves would be bothered by what the two little girls were about to do.

Even though Nabby was twelve years old and Betty only nine, their futures were already more or less set out for them. It was the 17th century, after all; practically all women had a similar fate—getting married and having children. Whether they were royal princesses or common folk like Betty and Nabby, society had decided this for them from the moment they were born and found to be female. Hence, these girls' dreams centered largely around their future husbands. Despite their young age, the two little girls were overwhelmed with curiosity about what their husbands would be like. Would they be handsome? Rich? Poor? Romantic? There was no way of knowing, at least not according to the adults, anyway. But Nabby had heard of something from the girls at school (or perhaps from Tituba herself)—a technique for telling the future. This form of fortune-telling was called the "Venus glass," and although Nabby instinctively knew that Reverend Parris would not allow them to try it, she figured that what the reverend didn't know couldn't hurt him.

The girls filled a glass of water. Giggling in nervous anticipation, they set the glass on the table. Nabby grabbed an egg and separated it carefully, allowing the white to fall into the water as she kept the yolk inside the shells. Once all the white was in the water, the two girls stared intensely into the glass. The girls at school had told them that the egg white would curl in the water and show them signs about their future husbands. Wide-eyed and pushing each other, the girls watched as the egg formed swirling shapes. Was that a coin? A wheel? A bird's wing? A stone? The girls were speculating wildly about the natures of their future husbands, about whether he would be rich, handsome, or kind.

And then they both saw it at the same time. The egg white became a shape, a terrifying shape that both the little girls recognized instantly. They'd seen that shape before, being lowered slowly into the ground. Perhaps Nabby had seen her deceased parents being lifted into one. And now, unmistakably, it curved in the water in front of their eyes.

A coffin.

The girls screamed. Tituba came running into the kitchen, but they had already fled, clattering up the stairs, shrieking all the way.

* * *

The symptoms started in January 1692, not long after the fortune-telling, and they were as cruel as they were perplexing.

Deodat Lawson, the former minister of Salem Village, was one of the first outsiders to witness the symptoms, and he was horrified by what he saw. The sweet, playful little girls in the parsonage where he had' once lived and worked were overcome by something so terrifying that, to Lawson, it looked otherworldly.

Nabby was the unlucky one who suffered the symptoms during Lawson's visit. Samuel, Elizabeth, and a wide-eyed Betty watched alongside Lawson in terror as the symptoms seized hold of her. Nabby's muscles were thrown into a spasm that made her scream in pain, viciously contorting her limbs, her muscles and sinews straining underneath her pretty frock. Then she lurched upright. Her muscles jerked and twitched as if being controlled by some sadistic puppet master, sending her reeling across the room. Her arms were thrown up in the air as if she thought she could fly, and spurts of nonsensical sounds spilled from her lips. The only words that made sense—and even those didn't make much sense—were when she was yelping in pain and then saying that someone had pinched her. There was nobody near her, and she insisted that she had been pinched by a spirit.

Reverend Parris crossed the floor toward Nabby, begging her to stop. She spun around to face him, her eyes suddenly wild. When she opened her mouth, no words came out. Instead, she barked—a strange, harsh sound coming from the mouth of an innocent, little girl.

Parris turned back to Lawson, grimly explaining how the symptoms had started. First, both girls had seemed to be sick; they said that they felt feverish, and Elizabeth and the reverend treated them with traditional home remedies as they would any other minor ailment among their children. But it didn't end there. Soon, the girls' behavior took a turn for the strange. They started by hiding under furniture. Then came the screams of pain, which appeared utterly random—and then the fits began.

Parris had read the pamphlets by Cotton Mather that gave instructions for helping people who were possessed in this way. He and Elizabeth had been praying for the girls, but nothing worked. There was little that they could do other than to call for a doctor, which they did in late February 1692.

The only doctor in town—and likely, although history does not name him, the doctor that examined the girls—was William Griggs. "Doctor" may have been too generous a description. This was a time long before doctors had to be licensed to practice; in fact, Griggs very likely didn't even go to medical school but taught himself a series of quack techniques instead. Whether it was Griggs or not who examined the girls, the physician's diagnosis was emphatic. "They are under an evil hand," he said. The girls were possessed: they were the victims of witchcraft.

* * * *

Reverend Parris was desperate to keep the diagnosis as quiet as he could. Scandalized by the very idea that such goings-on could affect his esteemed, straight and narrow household, he was determined to keep the word from getting out to his congregation. What on Earth would they say?

Unfortunately for Parris, this was practically impossible. Salem Village was tiny and filled with gossipers. The word spread like wildfire, and one of the first people who heard about it was Mary Sibley, a neighbor of the Parris'. Sibley was a well-meaning busybody who loved to meddle in other people's affairs, and this fascinating case of witchcraft would have had to be one of them.

Determined to help the girls, Sibley wanted to try an old remedy that was a part of English folklore, brought across from Great Britain alongside the Pilgrims. Not all of the English settlers in the New World had been perfect Puritans, as the old rituals and "white magic" still survived. She knew that the use of this "magic" would be frowned upon by Reverend Parris, so she directed her attention instead to his male slave, John Indian. Likely a native from the island of Barbados, Indian willingly obeyed Sibley's instructions. He was to take some rye flour, obtain some urine from the two afflicted girls, and then give the nasty mixture to his wife Tituba to bake. Once the cake—more of a hard biscuit, in reality—was made, it would be fed to a dog. The dog was then supposed to point to the witch that had accursed the two victims.

John Indian did as he was told, feeding the icky, urine-laced cake to a dog. Unfortunately for Sibley, the dog completely failed to point to anyone. Instead, all that happened was that the rumor of the witchcraft that had befallen the minister's niece and daughter began to spread wildly throughout the village.

It wasn't the only thing that was spreading. It seemed that witchcraft, like hysteria, was somehow contagious.

Chapter 4 – The Affliction of Elizabeth Hubbard

Elizabeth Hubbard was an orphan and an outcast.

At seventeen years old, she knew that she would soon be of marriageable age. She also knew that practically nobody would want to marry her. During this period in history, women almost always came with considerable dowries—material wealth that brides would give to their husbands when they got married—which consisted of either money or property. Elizabeth had neither. In fact, she didn't even have parents; instead, she lived with her great-aunt Rachel Griggs and her great-uncle William, who was a doctor. The couple didn't treat her as an adopted daughter, however. Instead, Elizabeth was nothing more than a lowly maidservant to them. She scrubbed the floors and cleaned the dishes, and in exchange, she had a roof over her head and something to eat.

Elizabeth was well aware that her great-uncle was not a young man anymore. He was deep into his seventies by this time, and in the past few weeks, his face had grown more and more lined with each passing day. She guessed that it had something to do with the strange case that he was consulting on—a pair of girls whom, he said, were afflicted by witchcraft. The stories scared Elizabeth. Those contortions and strange behaviors were the stuff of nightmares.

The witchcraft cases had escalated in a single day. Now, a third young girl had been afflicted: Ann Putnam Jr. She was a part of the family that had become Reverend Parris' staunchest supporters and had also been a part of the fortune-telling escapades with Betty and Nabby. Now, Ann was suffering exactly the same symptoms. And these symptoms had also escalated. The "spirits" that were pinching and pricking the girls had taken form, and these terrorizing specters were none other than people that they recognized, figures from Salem Village.

It's uncertain what was going through Elizabeth's mind at this time. She may have been absolutely petrified of suffering the same curse that had befallen Betty, Nabby, and Ann Jr. But perhaps Elizabeth saw her chance to become more than just some maidservant. Either way, the result was the same: Elizabeth soon joined the ranks of the afflicted. She saw specters in her sleep and sometimes while she was awake too; they pinched her and pricked her with needles and screamed horrible, terrifying things at her as they swooped in and out of her vision. And they were familiar—terribly familiar. The faces of people she knew. The faces of people in Salem Village.

This was what she told Dr. Griggs in any case. Whether she truly was having these hallucinations or not, they caught the doctor's attention.

The entire village was starting to wake up to the strange events that were taking place in its streets. The tension that had always been rampant in the town had, in a matter of two or three days, turned into full-blown suspicion. The villagers knew that there was a witch in their midst, and every outsider had suddenly become more than the center of gossip—they had become suspects. Reverend Lawson was a guest speaker at the church shortly after his visit to see Nabby and Betty in their affliction, and his sermon was nothing short of a disaster: the four afflicted girls had awful, loud fits while he was speaking, bursting out with cries of pain and blasphemy, their bodies contorting, their voices shrieking in a way that made cold shivers run down Lawson's spine.

There was no doubt that there was trouble in Salem—big trouble. And because Elizabeth Hubbard was older than the other girls, her testimony was taken the most seriously. In fact, Elizabeth would go down in history as the main instigator of the trials themselves. The person who started it all.

* * * *

Betty Parris was the first person to point out a suspect. Since her diagnosis, the petrified nine-year-old had been under unrelenting pressure to tell her father—and the group of powerful villagers surrounding him—who exactly had afflicted her. Reverend Parris had publicly denounced Mary Sibley's use of the witch cake to find the culprits, but he was nonetheless determined to find the witch of Salem Village and prosecute that person for afflicting his little girl.

Little Betty's hallucinations had left her scared witless. Her father's gruff and angry manner was no help, either; she felt trapped, forced to point out someone who could have afflicted her. It is likely that Betty fully believed that she'd been cursed by a practitioner of dark magic, and she must have been frightened beyond description. She confessed to her father about the Venus glass, and his reaction would have probably been furious that his daughter would even dare to engage in fortune-telling. This was no help to the terrified Betty, and when her father continued to bully her into telling him who had done this to her, her thoughts went to one person: Tituba.

Tituba just about fit the bill in Betty's young mind. She was different, for a start, and therefore scary; it's also possible that she was the one who had taught the girls to use the Venus glass. Tituba wasn't a lifelong churchgoing Christian like most of the villagers. Instead, she had probably brought her beliefs with her from Barbados, which had a rich and extensive folklore largely centered on keeping ghosts—called duppy—away from the living. Besides, Betty may have reasoned, Tituba was just a slave, a slave who told her stories about spirits and superstitions. Pushed to make an accusation, Betty could think of no one else.

Elizabeth Hubbard was quick to back Betty up. At seventeen, her testimony held much more weight than those of either Betty or Nabby, and when she indicted Tituba as well, the people of Salem were quick to believe her. Tituba was just as much of an outsider to them as she was to Elizabeth and Betty. Pressured further, the four girls accused two more women: Sarah Good and Sarah Osborne.

Although both the women were white and English, they bore a strong similarity to Tituba in one noteworthy way: they were outsiders too. Good was a beggar, a destitute woman who used to go from house to house asking for food and shelter. She had a reputation for undesirable behavior, and when approached by the village's children (usually to mock her), she tended to treat them harshly. This was probably in self-defense, but it made her a frightening figure to the little girls of the village.

Sarah Osborne had broken many cultural norms for love. She'd been married to a relative of the powerful Putnam family, Robert Prince. When Prince passed away, he left his lands to his two young sons, with Osborne caring for them until the boys were of age. Instead of doing as her late husband had desired, however, Osborne remarried—and her new husband was not a respectable person like Prince had been. Instead, William Osborne was a former indentured servant, a nobody. She gave Prince's lands to him and thus earned the contempt of the Putnams. It may have been no coincidence that little Ann Putnam Jr. was one of her accusers.

Whatever reasons the accusers had, the results were the same: Good, Osborne, and Tituba had all become leading suspects. And even though there was no evidence against them but the testimony of four girls—the eldest of whom was just seventeen—the Putnams and Reverend Parris had decided that arrests had to be made.

Chapter 5 – The Confession of Tituba

Magistrate John Hathorne was so severe a man that he had more or less made a career out of it. A captain of the military during King Philip's War, he was a ruthless businessman, a harsh judge, and an avid prosecutor of the Quakers. If it didn't conform to his ideas, he was very ready to destroy it. And Tituba, standing before him, very much did not conform. Her strange accent and stumbling English were a condemnation already, but she was a slave, which was bad, and black, which was even worse. But none of this could touch the fact that the slave woman had been accused of witchcraft. In Hathorne's eyes, she was already guilty.

Hathorne hardly gave Tituba any chance to defend herself. He leaned forward, his steely eyes boring into the frightened face of the young slave woman. Although she would later be depicted in popular culture as a scary old hag, Tituba was no older than her early twenties at the time of the trials.

"Tituba," Hathorne spat. "What evil spirit have you familiarity with?"

Tituba was trembling where she stood. Hathorne was not so much a judge as he was yet another accuser. Only one word slipped out of her mouth. "None."

Hathorne frowned at her insolence. “Why do you hurt these children?” he demanded, ignoring the fact that she was little older than her so-called victims.

“I do not hurt them,” Tituba whispered, not daring to lift her eyes to his.

Sitting back, Hathorne snorted. “Who is it then?” he demanded, snidely.

Tituba swallowed hard. She had faced many hardships in her life, but this ’might have been the worst of them all. Presumably born in Barbados, Tituba was of native descent. She’d been sold as a slave to the frightening Samuel Parris when she was just a little girl, probably no older than twelve, alongside a young man her age and a boy who was even younger. The three of them had been shipped to Boston when Parris had abandoned his Barbados plantation and moved to Massachusetts, and it can only be presumed that the journey had been frightening and arduous. Tituba had had no say in her own fate; she’d simply been dragged along with her master because she was just property to him, like a table or a carriage or a cow. She had married John Indian—which was probably not his birth name, just what the white men called him—and they were still with Parris in Salem Village, but the African slave boy who’d come to Boston with them was dead. Now, she found herself accused of witchcraft, something that she possibly barely understood.

It’s said that Parris had beaten her after Betty’s accusation, ordering her to confess. Other historians allege that Tituba’s testimony was a trick, a crafty bid for freedom. Yet either way, standing before the terrifying Hathorne, with the memory of her recent beating still throbbing in the welts on her back and shoulders, the slave woman must have been scared out of her skin.

She took a deep breath and responded to Hathorne’s question with the fateful words. “The devil,” she said, with the bravado of the other side of fear, “for ought I know.”

Hathorne’s eyes intensified. “Did you never see the devil?”

Tituba looked up. The sentence that she uttered next would change history—or at least, it would change the history of Salem Village and turn it into a scene of tragedy forever.

"The devil came to me," she told Hathorne. "And bid me serve him."

Hathorne sat back. He had struck gold: he had gotten a confession out of the hated slave woman, and it was now official. Salem Village was home to a witch. But Hathorne believed that there was more than one witch involved, so his next question was, "Who have you seen?"

Tituba told him everything—everything that would make the villagers' hair stand on end in terror as they listened to her testimony. She told him that there were five other witches who were afflicting the children and that two of them were Sarah Good and Sarah Osborne, the same women that the girls had also accused. Apparently, these five witches had been the ones to force Tituba to do what she had done to Betty, Nabby, and the others. "[They] lay all upon me and they tell me if I will not hurt the children they will hurt me," she stammered in her poor English. Hathorne asked her if she was sorry that she'd hurt the children; she responded that she was but insisted that the other witches would have done something terrible to her if she didn't do as they'd told her.

Then the examination took a terrifying turn. Hathorne asked Tituba again what she had seen, and she responded that a man had come to her and told her to serve him. Possibly presuming that the man she was indicating was one of the other witches, Hathorne pressed her for more information.

"Last night there was an…appearance," Tituba said. "It said, 'Kill the children.'"

Appearance? Chills ran down Hathorne's spine. "What is this 'appearance' that you see?" he asked.

This was where Tituba's testimony truly crossed over into supernatural territory in the eyes of the residents of Salem Village.

"Sometimes it is like a hog," she said, "and sometimes like a great dog." She went on to describe chilling encounters with this so-called specter: it was sometimes a pig, sometimes a black dog, sometimes a man that tried to seduce her with "pretty things" like a yellow bird. Sometimes there were rats—one red, one black. All of the specters had two things in common: they all told her to serve them and threatened her with harm if she didn't, and they all scared her.

Her story continued, growing more and more twisted. She confessed to pinching Elizabeth Hubbard and to stabbing Ann Putnam Jr. with some kind of a spectral knife, and she made Good and Osborne out to be even worse than she was. She told Hathorne that the two other women were strong witches that transformed into horrible specters—winged creatures, hairy creatures, strange two-legged creatures, a man dressed in black with white hair, a woman in a white hood with a topknot—and that they rode on "sticks" and set spectral wolves upon their victims.

Hathorne knew that Tituba had condemned herself by her own confession. There was only one thing left that he needed out of her: information to condemn Good and Osborne, too.

"Do you see who it is that torments these children now?" he asked, soft as a prowling tiger.

"Yes," said Tituba, her voice faint and trembling with terror. "It is Good. She hurts them in her own shape."

Hathorne wanted more. "And who is it that hurts them now?"

But Tituba was done. She was overwhelmed by what she had just told Hathorne, whether it had all been a fabrication or some elaborate hallucination that she herself had suffered.

"I am blind now," she said, ending the testimony that would rock the history of America forever. "I cannot see."

Chapter 6 – Fuel on the Fire

Illustration II: An engraving from William A. Crafts' Pioneers in the Settlement of America shows one of the afflicted girls in the midst of a fit during the examination of a suspected witch

https://commons.wikimedia.org/wiki/File:SalemWitchcraftTrial_large.jpg

Tituba's historic confession took place somewhere between March 1st and March 7th. A warrant for her arrest—and the arrests of Good and Osborne—had been issued on February 29th, and John Hathorne, along with his colleague Jonathan Corwin (the same Corwin that owned Salem's so-called Witch House), spent a full week interrogating them.

Tituba's words served like fuel on a wildfire. To have people being accused of witchcraft in the village was one thing; to actually have them confess was another. Soon, child after child was falling dramatically ill with the same symptoms that had afflicted little Betty Parris. Paranoia became rampant, stalking the streets, making every outsider look suspicious. The fact that Good and Osborne both vehemently denied any involvement in the witchcraft that Tituba had so freely described mattered little. They were guilty in Hathorne's and Corwin's eyes.

Good, Osborne, and Tituba were all interrogated for a full week before being imprisoned, awaiting their trials. But the hunt was far from over. From Tituba's confession, Hathorne knew that he was looking for at least three more witches—and he would not rest until he'd found them.

* * * *

Ann Putnam Jr. would be the next to make an accusation. The thirteen-year-old eldest daughter of Ann Putnam Sr. and Thomas Putnam, young Ann had grown up in an environment of strife and contention. The Putnams had been living in Salem for so long that they felt like they owned the place; they were also allies of Reverend Parris and locked in a decades-long feud with the nearby Proctor family over the borders of their lands. In short, the Putnams were troublemakers—powerful troublemakers, and not only in their community. They were abusive in the home as well.

Little Ann was tormented by the memory of her infant sister. Sarah Putnam had been only six weeks old when she had died; Ann would later accuse one of the so-called witches of beating her to death. In fact, history suggests that it's far more likely that Ann Putnam Sr. had committed the atrocious deed of whipping a tiny baby to death. It's been speculated that Ann Jr.'s testimonies were misplaced anger, the result of a teenage girl who had been mistreated for all of her life.

Either way, Ann was the first girl to point the finger at a member of the church itself. Martha Corey and her husband Giles had been full members of the church for some time, but that didn't mean that they weren't outsiders. In fact, Martha was one of the most scandalous people in Salem, according to the church. Giles was her second husband but definitely not just the second man that she'd ever been with; during her first marriage to Henry Rich, she'd given birth to a son whose skin was nowhere close to the white tone of either Martha or Henry. This mulatto son was likely half-Native American, and his name was Benjamin or Benoni. Martha was promptly thrown out of Henry Rich's house; her legitimate son to Henry would stay with his father while Martha raised Benoni.

In 1690, following the death of Henry Rich, Martha married Giles Corey and moved in with him, taking Benoni with her. In Salem Village, adultery was a scandal all by itself; committing adultery with a non-white person was on a whole different level. Martha might have been a part of the church, but she was the topic of much gossip, and she became Ann Jr.'s next target.

It started when Giles, curious about the chaos that had suddenly overtaken the village, suggested that he and Martha attend one of the trials that was taking place that evening. Martha stubbornly refused, an act that would have been rare in that time—wives were expected to be obedient and submissive to their husbands. It was well known in the village that Giles and Martha didn't get along, and their latest argument was no surprise, but Giles made matters worse by bemoaning his wife's stubbornness to his neighbors. When word got out that Martha didn't want to attend the trials—which, by this time, had become something of a spectator sport in sleepy Salem—she was immediately the subject of suspicion.

Ann Jr. told authorities on March 12th that she'd seen the specter of Martha Corey, or at least the records reflect that Ann Jr. did. Her father, Thomas, was the one who submitted the deposition; in fact, Thomas and his brother Edward submitted almost all of the girls' official complaints, considering that none of them were of age. It has been suggested that Thomas manipulated the records, too. Either way, Martha was arrested, and she was quickly followed by Rebecca Nurse.

Unlike the other accused, Rebecca was a well-liked old lady and a beloved part of the community. She was a grandmother and seventy years old by the time she was accused, as sick as she was elderly. Dragged to the church building to be examined—the courthouse was too small to hold the massive audience that gathered with morbid curiosity to watch the trials—Rebecca was a frail, little figure cowering in the big building as Nabby Williams testified against her. Nabby reported that Rebecca's specter had terrorized her that very morning. Before Hathorne could turn his attention to Rebecca, Ann Jr., who was watching, fell to the ground. Her limbs contorted, her mouth stretched wide in a panicked scream, and a hush of terror fell upon the gathered people. Surely, innocent as the old lady looked, she must be afflicting young Ann right before their very eyes.

Poor old Rebecca was doomed even before her examination took place. The afflicted—who now included at least two more girls, Mary Walcott and Mary Warren—were watching eagerly as Hathorne set his first question to the old lady. "Are you an innocent person relating to this witchcraft?" he asked.

Rebecca was shaky and slow. She began to answer, but before she could get the words out, a terrible shriek rose up from the group of afflicted girls. "Did you not bring the Black Man with you?" howled Ann Putnam Sr., watching as her daughter writhed on the floor in agony. Hathorne's tone turned accusatory, and Rebecca could do nothing to defend herself, even though the congregation protested that she had to be innocent.

It mattered little that Rebecca asserted her innocence over and over, even suggesting that the devil was appearing in her image but that she had nothing to do with it. Nor did it matter how well-liked she was. The witchcraft hysteria had grown far beyond simply getting rid of some outsiders, and when Rebecca was held for trial alongside Martha Corey and long-time Putnam enemy John Proctor, it became obvious to the people of Salem that things had gone much further than they had expected.

And they were about to go further still.

Chapter 7 – The Madness Intensifies

By March 23rd, a little less than a month after Betty and Nabby were first diagnosed with witchcraft, there were six people languishing in jail for witchcraft: Tituba, Sarah Good, Sarah Osborne, Rebecca Nurse, Martha Corey, and John Proctor. The youngest of these was Tituba, who might have even been in her late teens herself. Some of them were outcasts, and one was a sweet little old lady who didn't deserve to be lying in the dismal and rat-infested cells. But none of them had guessed how awful their story was about to become—or that their next fellow prisoner would also be so desperately undeserving of arrest.

Sarah Good had nothing—a former husband, Daniel Poole, whose debt had left her impoverished, no home, no friends, no extended family, and most of the time, nothing even to eat. Although she had remarried to William Good, their relationship wasn't very solid. The only thing in the world that she could call her own was her four-year-old daughter, Dorothy.

Even Dorothy, however, was not safe. On March 24th, Hathorne issued a warrant for her arrest—a ridiculous thing considering that the little girl was only four years old. It was less of an arrest than it was a simple kidnapping of the tiny child, who was brought before the judges to be interrogated just like her mother. Unfortunately for

Dorothy, instead of the interrogation lasting for only seven days, hers went on for nearly two weeks. Mercy Lewis, Mary Walcott, and even Ann Putnam Jr. accused Dorothy of performing witchcraft. They told the judge that the little girl had been biting them like some rabid animal, even showing the little bite marks on their bodies to "prove" it. They claimed that Dorothy had tried to choke them, pinch them, beat them, and had continually demanded them to sign the devil's book.

Poor little Dorothy was scared witless. First, she had been living on the streets with her parents to start with, homeless and destitute—not exactly an idyllic life for anyone, let alone a child. Then strangers had come to drag her mother away, telling everyone that she was a witch, and Dorothy—who probably had a childish belief in witches—didn't know what to think. When they came for her, she was almost incoherent with terror. Facing Hathorne's cold questioning, Dorothy asserted her innocence courageously for a full two weeks, but at the beginning of April, she finally confessed. She likely did so because she hoped to be taken to be with her mother if she was also found guilty.

Little Dorothy was left to languish in a jail cell, pending a bail of fifty pounds, a truly insurmountable sum of money for her 17th-century beggar of a father. Jail today would be torture for a child; jail 400 years ago was almost unbearable. She was cold, scared, starving, and sick, and she was as innocent as could be.

* * *

Perhaps it was the arrest and trial of poor little Dorothy Good that caused Mary Warren to suddenly change her mind—or it could have been the overbearing presence of her skeptical master.

Possibly born in 1674, Mary Warren was the oldest of the accusers, as she was eighteen years old. She had lost her entire family when she was just a little girl, but 17th-century Massachusetts made little allowance for orphans; Mary had no choice but to become a servant. In reality, she was little more than a slave to the Proctor family.

Mary's fits started in March. Her symptoms were all but identical to those of the other girls: she screamed and contorted and yelled out in terror about strange things that she was seeing and feeling. Her master, John Proctor, may have been one of the only people in Salem left with a grain of sense, or perhaps he was just immune to the mass hysteria that had gripped the village. He saw the accused girls' testimonies as completely fake, declared loudly to his family that the girls should be whipped for lying and wasting people's time, seeing the trials as a bid by his rivals, the Putnams, to seize more power in the village. When Mary started having fits, Proctor was incensed. He accused her of lying and assured her that he wouldn't fall for that nonsense. In fact, he gave her extra work to do behind the spinning wheel and told her that if she tried it again, he would give her a sound whipping.

Mary's protestations that the specter terrorizing her was that of Giles Corey, the husband of the jailed Martha Corey, fell on deaf ears. Proctor kept her so busy that no further fits befell her for weeks, and on April 2nd, Mary posted a note on the door of the church building thanking the congregation for praying for her. The community, desperate to figure out how to get the afflicted girls' torments to stop, questioned Mary about what had happened.

The questioning took a completely different line than what the community had expected. When they asked her how she had gotten rid of the affliction, Mary insinuated that there had never been any affliction at all—in fact, between the lines, she accused the other girls of lying about the whole thing. The village was shocked, and for a moment, it seemed that they would accept that Mary was telling the truth. She was the oldest of the afflicted girls, after all, and many of them—such as Elizabeth Hubbard, Nabby Williams, and Mary herself—had reason to lie.

Just as the congregation was beginning to think that they had overreacted, however, the other afflicted girls retaliated. Mary's flash of insight or honesty backfired badly on her when, on April 18th, the other afflicted girls filed a formal complaint against her.

Now, Mary was no longer simply afflicted—she was considered a witch herself.

By this time, John Proctor and his wife Elizabeth were also suspects and being interrogated for witchcraft. Nabby Williams, Ann Putnam Jr., and Mary Warren had all implicated them (Mary before being accused herself), and when Nabby was allowed to question Elizabeth Proctor, she insinuated that the older woman had been using Mary to carry out some of her dirty work. Mary was arrested and interrogated, but the interrogation didn't go well; she was vague, constantly gripped by fits, and only managed to briefly allude to some of the other witches—notably the Proctors—forcing her into carrying out some of their work. Mary was ultimately pardoned, but her testimony steeped the Proctors in guilt. The triumphant Putnams watched, proudly supporting Ann Jr., as the Proctors were led away in chains. Ann Jr. followed this up by saying that she, too, had been terrorized by the specter of Giles Corey.

By the time Mary was released, many more people had been accused of witchcraft—in fact, the circle of suspects had grown far beyond the original five that Tituba had implicated. The list of suspects now included Sarah Cloyce, Rebecca Nurse's sister, who had tried to defend poor old Rebecca; Giles Corey; John and Elizabeth Proctor; Abigail and Deliverance Hobbs; Bridget Bishop; and Mary Eastey.

The stain of the hysteria was spreading rapidly throughout Salem Village, like blood in the water. But nobody could have guessed that the next person to be accused would be a minister.

Chapter 8 – The Reverend in League with the Devil

Handsome in a swarthy way, as confident as they come, and educated at Harvard, Reverend George Burroughs had always been a popular man.

His childhood, however, had not been easy. He was born either in Suffolk, England, or Scituate, Massachusetts, sometime in 1650. His mother raised young George in a pious household, which eventually spurred him to become a minister.

By all accounts, Burroughs quickly proved himself to be an able minister. His people called him generous, good, and hardworking, although some sources say that his wives' opinions of him were quite different, mainly that they were harshly treated. And he had several of them. He married Hannah Fisher when he was in his twenties and served as a minister in Maine. There, he and Hannah were forced to survive a devastating attack by French-supported Native Americans during King Philip's War. The bloody fight left 32 settlers dead and their settlement destroyed. Burroughs took his family and fled south, hoping to escape the marauding hordes. He eventually landed in the contentious little village of Salem.

Burroughs was appointed as the minister of Salem, although he quickly found out how difficult the villagers would be. The village contended with him over his salary, and he wasn't even given a parsonage to stay in; instead, he found himself lodging with none other than part of the Putnam family. While he was staying there, Burroughs lost his wife, Hannah, during childbirth. He was left with their nine children, including Hannah's surviving newborn. Marrying a rich widow named Sarah Ruck Hathorne (the former wife of Captain William Hathorne, who was the father of Judge John Hathorne, the same man who would later interrogate George Burroughs), Burroughs was kicked out of the community by the angry villagers who still refused to pay his salary. He moved back toward Maine and quickly regretted it when Native American raids once again plagued him and his family.

Burroughs, however, survived the raids, unlike the parents of a young girl named Mercy Lewis. The Lewis family had traveled closely with the Burroughs family, and when most of them were killed in an attack by Native Americans, young Mercy was sent to stay with the Burroughs family as a servant. Much like Elizabeth Hubbard and Mary Warren, Mercy was little more than a slave and was possibly ill-treated by Burroughs.

Eventually, unwilling to bear the struggle with him any longer, Mercy traveled back to Salem with some other refugees. She became a servant of the Putnam family, and she was in her late teens when the affliction started. She likely lived quite closely with Ann Jr., and it didn't take long before she was suffering exactly the same symptoms.

* * * *

It was April 30th, and the debacle had been dragging on for two long months. No one had yet been tried, but many of the accused were waiting in jail as the constable continued to make arrest after arrest and the afflicted continued to make their complaints of supernatural torment. Hathorne and the other judges were after one person, though: the man dressed in black that the girls had all been speaking of. Some suspected that this figure was the devil himself, but others, seeing the size of the witchcraft spectacle, presumed that there had to be a ringleader somewhere. There had to be someone who was organizing this—it was on far too large a scale to be a random effort, the community theorized.

And when Mercy Lewis first began to tell the people that she had seen the specter of none other than George Burroughs, it began to make sense to many members of the congregation. Burroughs had left the congregation with his tail between his legs, hounded off because of the dispute over his salary. While he certainly had some allies, who had helped to pay off the debt he incurred while arranging Hannah's funeral, he also undoubtedly had a large number of enemies. He had also never been officially ordained as a minister.

Burroughs was sitting at dinner with his family when officers from Portsmouth charged into his house. Burroughs was startled to see them and, it is presumed, put up something of a struggle, but it was no good. The officers seized him, and he was more or less dragged back to Salem. On their way back to the village, a mighty thunderstorm took place, which the frightened officers took to be Satan's attempt at rescuing his minion.

It seemed like no one was safe from witchcraft. No one could be considered innocent based on their occupation or social standing. An honest-to-goodness church minister had been arrested, and his arrest meant that nobody was off-limits to the accusers.

Burroughs was examined on May 9th, 1692. His relative by marriage, John Hathorne, was among the judges that delivered the interrogation. Their suspicions were based not only on the accusations of the afflicted girls but also on the fact that Burroughs had lost two of his wives—both Hannah Fisher and Sarah Ruck Hathorne were dead, and he had recently married a third wife, Mary, whose maiden name is unknown. Burroughs was accused of using witchcraft to murder his previous wives. This accusation was supported by Ann Putnam Jr., who told the magistrates that she had seen two women dressed in shrouds appear to her, telling her about how they had been brutally killed by their diabolical husband. The women were presumed to be Hannah and Sarah Burroughs.

Burroughs' examination also took a turn for the downright strange, if these witch trials could conceivably get any stranger. He was accused of having superhuman strength. Having above-average physical strength was an unusual trait for a Puritan minister in any case; they were usually somewhat underfed, pale, scholarly types that spent hours poring over the Bible, not hefting heavy loads out in the field like many of the members of their flock. But Burroughs was different. It was said that he could carry huge loads over long distances without any help, that he could travel as fast as a horse, and that he could lift a heavy musket with only his finger crooked into the barrel. When Burroughs protested that he "achieved" the aforementioned feats with the help of a Native American companion—likely a servant—the judges were quick to assert that his "companion" must have been the devil himself.

Burroughs was jailed, and two days later, Margaret Jacobs—who had been accused as well—confessed to being a witch. By this time, word had gotten out that witches who confessed would not be executed; for many of the accused, it would have seemed like the only way to escape with their lives. Jacobs, however, also implicated two men in helping her with the witchcraft she performed: her father George Jacobs and the minister George Burroughs.

The judges rejoiced, believing that they had discovered the leader of the witchcraft group. It mattered little that Burroughs continued to protest his innocence. He was jailed awaiting trial and subjected to a humiliating physical examination in which his entire body was inspected for any marks or blemishes. If marks were found, they were pricked with a pin to see if blood came out; if there was no blood, the marks were presumed to be the stamp of Satan. No witch's marks were found on Burroughs, but he was thrown in jail again, nevertheless.

Chapter 9 – The First Casualty

Accusations continued to stream in throughout the month of April. Practically no evidence was required to make an arrest; an accusation, and that from a minor, with only spectral evidence—evidence from a dream or vision—was quite enough. Salem Village's little jail was soon filled to overflowing.

A surprising number of people confessed to the diabolical actions of which they were accused. And almost every person that confessed implicated more and more accomplices—some who had not yet even been considered as suspects. Abigail and Deliverance Hobbs confessed around the same time as Mary Warren, and they started naming several people who had apparently worked with them to afflict the children, including Deliverance's own husband, William (Abigail's father). Edward and Sarah Bishop, Mary English, and Nehemiah Abbott Jr. were among the accused as well.

Burroughs was not the only person to be arrested on April 30th, either. He came to Salem to find a whole group of people who had been arrested on the same day, including Susannah Martin, Sarah Morey, Dorcas Hoar, and Mary English's husband, Philip.

This influx of newly accused people and their long and dramatic interrogations meant that the actual trials of those who had already been examined were being postponed. The first three suspects—

Tituba, Sarah Good, and Sarah Osborne—had, by mid-May, been languishing in jail for more than two full months.

Tituba, who was young and used to hardship, having lived the dismal life of a slave, was more or less all right. But the other two women were suffering. Sarah Good had to deal with the fact that poor little Dorothy was still languishing in jail; she had not been placed in a cell with her mother as she'd hoped but was all by herself in some dark, rank corner. She had no company, no one to play with, and no one to care for her. The little girl was retreating further and further into the recesses of her troubled mind.

But that wasn't all that Sarah Good was struggling with. Sarah was pregnant. She was expecting a sibling for Dorothy, and as her time in jail dragged on, her belly continued to swell. Finally, the day came for her to deliver her little baby. The conditions in the jail were appalling—cold, bare, and filthy—and she was possibly not given any assistance except by her cellmates, who may have been Sarah Osborne and Tituba. Considering that the three women had been implicating each other in their interrogations, there was no love lost between them, either. Alone and struggling, Sarah finally produced a baby girl. Perhaps in the sad hope that the justice system would finally see some sense, she named the infant Mercy.

The justice system did not see sense. And baby Mercy never got to see the sunlight. Cold, hard, dirty, cruel jail was no place for a sweet, soft little baby girl. She didn't live long. Mercy died in Sarah's arms, and she took all hope of mercy from the judges with her.

Sarah Osborne was doing little better than her fellow accused. A fairly elderly woman for that era at 49 years of age, Osborne had not been well to begin with, having missed out on going to church for years as a result of illness. Her illness was only getting worse in the cold, damp jail. The healthcare of that time had been utterly ineffective in helping her, and even that was not afforded to her in jail. She was a witch, after all; she was more than likely destined to hang anyway. Perhaps hanging would have been a far simpler and less painful way to die than to waste away, inch by inch, her disease slowly overcoming her until she was just a withered skeleton. She breathed her last on May 10th, 1692. Together with baby Mercy Good, Sarah Osborne became one of the first real victims of the Salem witch trials.

* * * *

William Phips had just become governor of Massachusetts Bay Colony, and he was determined—like Samuel Parris had been with Salem Village—to whip it into shape.

Shepherd, captain, treasure hunter, knight—Phips had worn a lot of different hats by the time he became the new governor. He grew up tending sheep on his father's farm in a distant corner of New England, just another illiterate kid in the colonies. He managed to wriggle his way onto a ship for the first time as a ship's carpenter in Boston as a young adult. From there, he gradually climbed the ranks until he finally succeeded in becoming the captain of his own ship. His goal was to seek Spanish treasure in the Caribbean. He and his crew were lucky enough to stumble upon the wreck of the *Concepcion*, from which they seized hundreds of thousands of pounds. While Phips could easily have disappeared into thin air with more than enough money to keep him satisfied for the rest of his life, he went to England instead and handed over his booty to the Crown. He was rewarded with a knighthood and a quite adequate fortune.

By 1691, Phips had made friends with some influential men in Massachusetts, including Reverend Increase Mather, the president of Harvard College, and his son, Cotton. The political advantage of knowing the Mathers assisted in getting Phips the position as governor. He returned to Massachusetts from London on May 14th, bringing with him the new Massachusetts Charter.

The new charter established Massachusetts as a province of Great Britain, no longer merely a colony. And Phips was the first governor who had been appointed by the king and queen. Massachusetts would no longer enjoy the independence it had formerly known, making it the beginning of the end for the witchcraft trials.

At first, however, Phips supported the trials. In fact, it was less than two weeks after he had arrived back in Boston that he decided that something would need to be done about the chaos in Salem. Instead of putting an end to the madness, Phips decided that the overwhelmed justice system in the village simply needed a little help to get the trials over with more quickly, especially considering that more and more accused were still streaming into the jail. He appointed a Court of Oyer and Terminer—a Court to Hear and Decide—to sort out the mess in Salem. This court was staffed by seven judges instead of the two who had been trying to deal with the accusations by themselves. John Hathorne was among these judges, as was Lieutenant Governor William Stoughton. Stoughton was Phips' first mistake; he was a devout Puritan who strongly believed in witchcraft and was just as biased toward the afflicted girls as Hathorne was. Phips' second mistake was in allowing spectral evidence to be used in the Court of Oyer and Terminer, despite the fact that both Increase and Cotton Mather had cautioned against its use. "It were better that ten suspected witches should escape, than that one innocent person should be condemned," Increase implored.

His plea fell upon deaf ears. The trials would go on—and they were about to get bloody.

Chapter 10 – Hanging

Summer had come to New England. The landscape that had still been blanketed in snow when Nabby Williams and Betty Parris first displayed symptoms of witchcraft was now a verdant green. Birds sang cheerfully in all of the trees, and the warm, bright sunshine that poured down upon the gathered crowd was intense.

It was a perfect summer's day. Not a breath of wind stirred the green foliage; the cascade of sunlight was hot and golden. Yet a chill was running through the people gathered at Gallows Hill in Salem Village. Some icy specter walked from one to the other, running ghostly fingers down the backs of their necks. The people murmured and shuffled, wondering aloud if the devil himself was walking among them. But they may have been cursed by nothing more than their own fear.

Then there was the rattle of a horse cart. The cart drew to a halt at the bottom of the barren hill, which was carpeted now in grass and wildflowers. The guards got out, and a woman was manhandled out of the cart, being pushed and shoved in disgust. Bridget Bishop. A mutter of hate stirred the crowd. Not a single eye that rested upon her lonely figure held the tiniest shred of approval, nor had it ever. Bridget had a reputation—and it wasn't a good one. Long before the witchcraft craze had ever begun, she had proven herself to be an outcast. Her behavior stuck out among her strictly Puritan neighbors as strikingly as her bright red bodice did in comparison with the grays and blacks worn by the respectable women of the village. Bridget was known for throwing wild drinking parties in her house, parties that went on for much longer than was considered to be normal; she had been married three times, leaving a trail of dead husbands in her wake. Even though she had only been accused on April 16th, 1692—weeks after Tituba and the others were first implicated—Bridget had taken priority in the trials of the new Court of Oyer and Terminer once it was formed at the end of May. She was the most important suspect for one reason: none of the other accused had quite so many people ready and willing to testify against them.

This was not Bridget's first witchcraft trial. She had been accused of killing one of her former husbands, Thomas Oliver, by witchcraft. While she was acquitted then, Bridget must have known, with the tension in Salem Village running as high as it was now, that she had little chance of escaping her fate this time.

The court had examined a large amount of spectral evidence when it came to Bridget. The afflicted girls testified much the same things about Bridget as they did about the other "witches": she bit and pinched them in her spirit form, and she tried to get them to sign or write in the devil's book. More serious evidence, however, was quickly brought forward as well. Some workmen told the court that they had found poppets in the cellar. Poppets are rag dolls that witches use to torment their victims, and to discover them in the walls of Bridget's cellar was a serious accusation indeed. Bridget denied any involvement with witchcraft, but she dug her own grave when she got carried away in her anger as she protested her innocence. "I am innocent to a witch," she shouted at the judge. "I know not what a Witch is."

The magistrate knew then that he'd ensnared her in her own words. "How can you know that you are no Witch, yet not know what a Witch is?" he demanded.

Bridget had no answer to that one. And so, on June 8th—less than two weeks after the Court of Oyer and Terminer was established—she found herself the first person to be formally indicted, tried, and sentenced for witchcraft. Of course, there could only be one sentence for such a heinous crime in the eyes of the colony.

It was June 10th. The day of her sentence. She walked up the long, barren hill among the angry mutters from the crowd surrounding her. The gallows had been built in eager anticipation of her death, and they waited for her at the top of the hill. Painted in golden sunlight, the noose hung waiting, motionless in the still air. The fact that Bridget was still a respected member of the church couldn't help her now. Nothing could help her now. She could only take one step at a time, experiencing her last minutes. Her last time walking. Her last time seeing the pure blue sky, the waving grass. Her last time feeling the summer air on her face and the ground beneath her feet. The last words she'd hear, the instructions of the guards to step up onto the platform. The last creak of wood. The last sensation, a rope around her neck.

A last glimpse at the village where she had lived, the village that had betrayed her. A last look into the faces of the staring crowd. A last breath.

Then the trapdoor fell. And Bridget Bishop, the first victim of the Salem witch trials, was hanged by the neck until dead.

* * * *

Roger Toothaker had been born in England, but North America was the only home he really knew.

One of the early English settlers of the New World, Toothaker had come across the great expanse of ocean aboard the *Hopewell* on September 11th, 1635. He was just a baby at the time, cradled in the arms of his mother. He lost his father as a toddler, but his mother remarried and rebuilt a life for herself and her children in Billerica, Massachusetts. Toothaker grew up to become a physician and folk healer whose specialty was hunting down witches. He could never have guessed that he would be condemned to death as one of them.

William Griggs was one of Roger Toothaker's greatest competitors in Salem Village and its neighbors. It may not be a coincidence, then, that Elizabeth Hubbard—Griggs' servant girl—was one of the people to accuse Toothaker of witchcraft in mid-May. Ann Putnam Jr. and Mary Walcott were also involved. It was the testimony of a young man named Thomas Gage, however, that would send Toothaker to jail. Gage told the court that Toothaker and his daughter had tried to fight fire with fire when it came to witches. They had used a black magic ceremony to kill a witch that was afflicting children in a similar manner to what the girls in Salem were experiencing.

It didn't matter that Toothaker had, allegedly, performed magic to kill a witch; doing magic at all made him a witch himself, and he was shipped off to jail without further ado to await trial and sentencing.

Jail proved to be its own sentence. Toothaker became the fourth victim of the witch trials on June 16th, 1692, just six days after Bridget Bishop hanged for her crimes. His death was ruled to be of natural causes, but one has to speculate that at his age—57—the conditions in jail may have contributed to those "natural" causes.

Toothaker was the fourth, but he was by no means the last of the victims. There would be more. Many, many more.

Chapter 11 – A Bid for Mercy

Illustration III: A 19th-century lithograph of an unnamed witch at a trial
https://commons.wikimedia.org/wiki/File:Salem_witch2.jpg

Mary Eastey was Rebecca Nurse's sister, and she seemed just as unlikely to be a witch as Rebecca was. But Rebecca, the elder of the two, had been trapped in a jail cell for weeks by the time Mary stood trial on May 31st, 1692.

Mary was well known in Salem Village for being a sweet and gentle soul. She was well into her fifties; everyone knew that she had a reputation for being as kind and patient as she was virtuous. The only blight that could have possibly been found in her record was that her mother, Joanna Blessing Towne (also a defender in the trials), had once been accused of witchcraft before. Mary and her sisters, Sarah Cloyce and Rebecca Nurse, had also been implicated, but it was soon discovered that their accusers had a personal agenda and no evidence to speak of, so all four women were released and their names cleared.

Things were different now, though. Now Salem was overcome with mania, and there would be no pardoning. Not even for poor Mary Eastey, wringing her hands as her accusers screamed and wailed that she was hurting them. In fact, in the very act of wringing her hands, Mary accidentally gave her accusers further opportunity to attack her. Mercy Lewis, seeing Mary interlacing her fingers, clasped her hands in the same gesture. Then she began to scream and stagger around the room, yelling in panic that she couldn't unlock her hands—they were stuck as if held there by a satanic hand. A thrill ran through the room as Mercy shrieked and stumbled about wildly. Horrified, Mary jumped back, her hands falling to her sides. When she did so, Mercy's hands were "freed." She gasped that Mary was afflicting her.

Worried though she was, Mary stood her ground with remarkable coherence and spirit. She shakily regained her composure as the magistrate turned on her. "What do you say?" he demanded. "Are you guilty?"

Mary raised her chin. "I can say before Christ Jesus, I am free," she said with resounding fearlessness.

The magistrate continued to question her, asking whether she complied with Satan. "I never complied with him," she asserted calmly, "but prayed against him all my days. I have no compliance with Satan in this. What would you have me do?"

The magistrate didn't care that Mary Eastey was innocent. He didn't care what she said either; he was just as overcome by the madness as the rest of Salem Village, and he refused to rest until he had her blood.

"Confess if you are guilty," he ordered.

Mary must have known that a confession would buy her freedom from the death penalty that was assuredly awaiting her if she continued to deny her involvement in witchcraft. But it mattered more to her to speak the truth than to stay alive. An aging lady who had seen too much death already, Mary refused to back down.

"I will say it, if it was my last time," she said, not cowed by the magistrate's angry glare. "I am clear of this sin."

"Of what sin?"

"Of witchcraft."

Something in Mary's fearless defense seemed to have made the judge a little doubtful. He stared at her, starting to feel a little confused. Turning to the accusers, he asked them hopefully, "Are you certain this is the woman?"

In response, the accusers threw themselves into a horrific set of fits. Their limbs twisted and bent the wrong way, their eyes popped, and they shrieked in horror and panic but couldn't emit a single coherent word. Their accusing glares were directed straight at Mary Eastey as they struggled.

Mary continued to assert her innocence until finally the magistrate gave up on getting her to confess. Indeed, she was released on May 18th, and for 48 glorious hours, she walked Salem Village as a free woman. But the reprieve was short-lived. Mercy Lewis continued, unrelentingly, to accuse Mary Eastey of tormenting her. On May 20th, Mary was arrested once again. And this time, she would not be released.

* * * *

Perhaps Mary's interrogation was one of the things that started to sway Nathaniel Saltonstall as he read through the records shortly after he was appointed as one of the judges to sit on the Court of Oyer and Terminer.

Mary Eastey's second stint in jail had lasted a week so far by the time the court was formed. Saltonstall, a true native of Massachusetts as he was born in the nearby village of Ipswich, had gained himself a seat on the Court of Oyer and Terminer not by his high rank but by his good reputation. A mere town clerk at the time the court was formed, Saltonstall had nonetheless proven himself by being firm yet kind wherever possible. Saltonstall may have already been angered by the cases of Mary Eastey, Rebecca Nurse, and others by the time he sat in on his first session with the Court of Oyer and Terminer. He still remained with the new court for about two weeks, however—possibly because he still occupied a relatively junior position as a town clerk instead of a magistrate and was keen for the opportunity to do something more prestigious. But as he watched the trial of Bridget Bishop, Saltonstall grew less and less enamored with the whole idea. He couldn't believe that spectral evidence—which even Cotton Mather, the man behind some of the reading material that had proven influential in turning people against so-called witches, had cautioned the court against—was being so freely admitted. He found the entire trial of Bridget Bishop detestable.

When Bishop was finally sentenced on June 8th, Saltonstall had had enough. In his mind, Bishop was innocent, and no amount of spectral evidence was going to convince him otherwise. By the time Bishop had been hanged two days later, Saltonstall had handed in his resignation. The judges wouldn't listen to him when he protested against the unjust ruling, and so, the only form of protest he had left was to walk away. He washed his hands of the madness in Salem and returned to his life as a town clerk.

If only the other judges in Salem had had one-half of the sense that Saltonstall had then perhaps there would not have been so much violence. But for some reason—whether it was personal ambition, genuine belief in witchcraft, mass hysteria, fear of the powerful players involved on the accusing side, or something else—the other judges stayed. They stayed, they judged, and they condemned.

Chapter 12 – The Reverend Hangs

Sarah Good had already lost everything. Her husband's debt had taken everything she owned materially. Poverty had ripped away any scrap of pride—and, according to some sources, sanity—that she had left. Her oldest child was slowly losing her mind alone in a jail cell; her youngest had lived for only a few blessed days before the conditions of that same jail overwhelmed her.

All that Sarah had was her life, and even that was about to be taken away from her. She walked up the same path that Bridget Bishop had trodden a little over a week ago, and this time, she wasn't alone. Four other women were walking alongside her. Susannah Martin, Elizabeth Howe, and Sarah Wildes were among them; Rebecca Nurse brought up the rear, slow and doddering, her old joints barely able to carry her frame, even though it was emaciated from months of suffering in jail.

Rebecca would likely have had the same fate as Sarah Osborne if the jury hadn't already condemned her to die. Her trial was a torturous thing, both for Rebecca and for the many people of Salem who genuinely liked her. In fact, she was so well supported that 39 people came together to sign a petition asking the court to release her, vouching for her good character. Among them, surprisingly, were even a few Putnams, despite the fact that Ann Putnam Jr. and her mother were Rebecca's lead accusers and that the Putnams had often faced her in court over land issues. The petitioners were aware that they were placing themselves in direct danger of being accused as witches by submitting the document, but they were determined to rescue the poor old lady from such a terrible fate.

The petition almost worked. The jury, after hearing Rebecca's case, returned their verdict as not guilty. The old lady on the stand must have felt an overwhelming rush of relief. Could she finally get back to her old life now? Would her twilight years be a time of peace in the freedom and security of her own home, surrounded by the many people that she loved?

It was not to be. When the jury foreman announced their verdict to the courtroom, a wail of panic rose up from the ranks of the accusers. They immediately fell into an unrelenting bout of fits, screaming that Rebecca was afflicting them. Their behavior moved William Stoughton, the Chief Justice, to ask the jury foreman to reconsider. He told the man to think about some of Rebecca's words when discussing another accused witch—the confessor, Deliverance Hobbs– referring to her as "one of us." The foreman returned to the jury. They likely knew that Rebecca and Deliverance were fellow villagers and could have even been friends before the trials. That "one of us" could have meant "one of the fellow accused" or even "one of the other people from Salem." But they took it to mean "a witch like me." And based on that tiny shred of evidence, the jury returned and demanded Rebecca to defend herself. It's uncertain whether Rebecca's deafness prevented her from replying or whether she had simply given up on living. Either way, a new verdict was returned: guilty.

A few days later, on July 3rd, Rebecca was taken to church for the last time. She had often sought solace in resting in its pews, but this time, no joy or compassion would be given to her. Instead, she was to suffer the pain and humiliation of being publicly excommunicated. And now, she was walking up Gallows Hill to be hanged as a witch at the age of 71.

Sarah Good had not had similar support at her trial. The verdict was guilty even before the trial began; there was no one to come to her defense, and she was in no state of mind to make any kind of a coherent defense herself. Her accusers would stop at nothing to see her hang, and neither would the court. Incredibly, one of the accusers was even proven to lie during the proceedings; she screamed that Sarah was stabbing her with a knife then produced a broken knife from somewhere on her person. A young man in the courtroom came forward with the rest of the knife, protesting that he'd thrown away the broken object and that the girl had fished it out of the garbage to use as fake evidence. The court, however, did not reconsider Sarah's verdict. The girl was simply given a figurative slap on the wrist for lying, and Sarah was condemned to die.

And die she did, along with the four other women on July 19th, 1692. But while Rebecca went to the gallows with the same morbid silence as she'd exhibited in the courtroom, Sarah was vociferously denying her involvement until the end. When a minister in the crowd, Nicholas Noyes, tried to make her confess even on the gallows, she lost her temper. "You are a liar!" she shrieked. "I am no more a witch than you are a wizard, and if you take away my life, God will give you blood to drink."

Sarah Good and the others were hanged. They died there on Gallows Hill, and many years later, Nicholas Noyes died too. He suffered an enormous internal hemorrhage and drowned in his own blood.

* * * *

"Our Father, who art in Heaven, hallowed be thy name."

The words were uttered in a ringing tone but one still disproportionate to the hush that fell upon the assembled villagers. The crowd surrounding the gallows was suddenly and completely silenced.

"Thy kingdom come. Thy will be done, on earth as it is in heaven."

The voice that spoke had preached often; yet more recently, it had been forced to testify in court. Once, it had rung out across the church in Wells, Maine, every Sunday morning, cajoling, chiding, and instructing the Puritan flock that resided there. A few days ago, it had been raised in temper, arguing innocence. And now, it concluded an epic speech fit for the pulpit but delivered at the gallows.

"Give us this day our daily bread; and forgive us our trespasses, as we forgive those who trespass against us…"

The absolute silence had become slightly broken now. The assembled crowd had come to watch a demon hang; they had not expected to hear a minister preach, but that was exactly what they heard on August 19th, 1692. And the sermon that had just been delivered to them had moved their hearts to such an extent that tears ran down the cheeks of the grown men who had gathered to watch George Burroughs die.

After Burroughs' arrest on April 30th, he had waited in jail for a full three months while the Court of Oyer and Terminer got its act together. He was tried on August 5th, where he was convicted based on the accounts of his superhuman strength, which was supposed to have come from the devil. Carried to Proctor's Ledge in a cart with four others—George Jacobs Sr., Martha Carrier, John Proctor, and John Willard—he had been more or less paraded through the jeering streets of Salem Village while the villagers hissed and booed at him, denouncing him as the leader of the satanic forces that had been afflicting them.

But when he was on the gallows, he delivered a speech to defend himself, and this time, his profession of innocence did not fall on deaf ears the way it had back in the courtroom. His stirring rendition of the Lord's Prayer, without hesitation from start to finish, had truly begun to affect the crowd. Cotton Mather, who was sitting on his horse nearby, watched in trepidation as the crowd began to murmur and shift uncomfortably. They had all once sat in the church house and listened to sermons from this man; he'd lived among them, and while they had fought over his salary, they also trusted him as their minister. And now, he'd just recited the Lord's Prayer, which no witch was supposed to be able to do. Despite the fact that the accusers, who were present, were shouting that Satan himself stood beside Burroughs, dictating the Lord's Prayer to him, the crowd was beginning to cry out for Burroughs to be pardoned. In fact, it looked as though they might organize a real resistance. The executioner was told to hurry. He dropped the trapdoor, and in seconds, it was too late for the crowd to do anything. George Burroughs was dead.

His death was almost an awakening from the stupor of hysteria that the citizens of Salem had been lost in for so long, a hysteria that had already taken seven lives by hanging—Burroughs was the eighth. The crowd started to question the decision to hang him. Seeing that trouble was brewing, Cotton Mather rode up on his horse and tried to reassure the crowd. Despite the fact that he had been so strongly against the use of spectral evidence in the witch trials, Cotton genuinely believed that Burroughs was a witch—considering that Burroughs had been convicted not only based on spectral evidence—and he was determined to convince the crowd that he was right. He reminded them that Burroughs was not an ordained minister and added that the devil could transform himself into the similitude of an angel if he so desired.

That did the trick. The crowd happily cut down Burroughs' body and dragged it across the rough ground so roughly that all of his clothes were torn away. Alongside some of the others, who were quickly hanged after him, he was tossed into a grave so shallow that his chin and one hand still protruded from the earth. No effort was made to bury him further. He was left that way for the wolves and the crows.

Chapter 13 – Crushed

Illustration IV: The death of Giles Corey as depicted in an 1892 edition of Witchcraft Illustrated. In reality, Corey's death more likely took place in a dark, empty room.
https://commons.wikimedia.org/wiki/File:Giles_Corey_restored.jpg

"More weight!"

The feeble voice was little more than a gasping echo in the dark room. It came from the mouth of the old man who lay on his back on the bare floor, stripped completely naked, and who was being slowly crushed to death.

A wooden plank had been laid across the length of the old man's body. There were rocks on the plank, great, heavy rocks that were slowly squeezing the life out of him. For two days, the Giles Corey had been told to make his plea before the court. For two days, he had continually refused. Every time he refused, a new rock was added. And now, it was evident that he couldn't take much more. How the frail old body had survived 48 hours of this horrific treatment was unclear, but it was obvious that it was failing now.

The old man was so pale, his lips so blue, that it seemed as though the rocks had squeezed the final dregs of his life out of him. But his eyes still flashed with fire when Sheriff George Corwin told him to plead guilty. "More weight!" he wheezed, his lungs almost flattened already. "More weight!"

Corwin's teeth were bared in anger. He knew that if this stubborn old man went to his grave without pleading one way or the other, then he would die without a guilty verdict—and his lands, which were considerable, would go to his two sons. If Giles Corey was found guilty, however, his lands would go to the state when he was executed, and Corwin had been happily feathering his nest with the property of dead witches. He wanted Giles Corey's lands, and he would do whatever it took to get them.

So, when the old man cried, "More weight!" Corwin complied. He leaped up onto the plank, adding his own considerable mass to the intolerable, crushing power of the boulders that had been slowly squeezing the life out of that old man for two days. The pressure on Corey's body was such that his tongue, parched and swollen with suffering from nothing to drink except three gulps of stagnant water for days, was forced out of his mouth. Corwin seized his cane and roughly jammed Corey's tongue back into his mouth. "Confess!" he shouted. "Confess!"

But Giles Corey was as proud as he was stubborn. He had been born in England in the summer of 1611, coming to Massachusetts as a young man to seek his fortune. And he certainly found it. Starting out as a poor farmer, he quickly built his lands and business to the point that he was one of the wealthier landowners in the Salem district. However, controversy had been surrounding Corey for some time. In 1675, almost twenty years earlier, Corey had discovered that one of his indentured servants was stealing apples from his barn. Corey's rage spilled over into brutal violence. He took his cane to the servant, the same way that Corwin had taken his cane to Corey's tongue, and beat him so badly that his injuries warranted hospitalization. Tragically, complications from the injuries—a blood clot that broke loose—killed the servant ten agonizing days later. Corey was accused of murder, but because he was a wealthy farmer and the victim was just a servant, he was allowed to buy his innocence by paying a fine. For a man of Corey's stature, the fine was little more than just a slap on the wrist.

His past had come back to haunt him, however. When his wife, Martha Corey, was first arrested, Giles Corey more or less left her to it. Their marriage was notoriously rocky; in fact, part of Martha's accusation was the fact that she hadn't wanted to go and watch some of the earliest trials, a fact that Giles made public. Despite the fact that there was little love lost between Martha and Giles, he was soon accused by Ann Putnam Jr., Abigail Williams, and Mercy Lewis, who testified that his specter had been visiting and attacking them. He stood trial in mid-September before the Court of Oyer and Terminer. By this time, eleven people had already been hanged on Gallows Hill. Now that Rebecca Nurse and George Burroughs, in particular, were dead, Corey knew that he didn't stand a chance against a court that had already decided he was guilty. So, he decided not to stoop to the indignity of even attempting to defend himself. Indeed, he decided not to say anything at all. He kept his mouth shut in the courtroom, refusing to plead either way. According to 17th-century law, Giles, therefore, would have to be forced to plead or he would have to die.

Despite the fact that he was around 81 years old by this time, Corey was sentenced to suffer the torture of *peine forte et dure*, or "hard and forceful punishment." This grotesque form of forcing a defendant to plead one way or the other was known simply as "pressing," and Corey endured it for two long days, starting on September 17th, 1692. But as Corwin bounced on the board that was pinning the old man's fragile body to the ground, Corey wouldn't have to endure it much longer. He was dying.

And he was not giving in. Corwin paused, giving the old man one last chance to plead either guilty or not guilty so that the trial could proceed. Struggling for each breath, his ribs shattered, his lungs half-crushed, Corey's popping eyes could no longer focus, but he could croak out two last words despite his bruised and bloodied tongue.

"More weight," he groaned. And then he died, on his own terms and in full possession of his estate, which was divided among his two sons instead of going to the greedy Corwin.

He was only fined for the brutal murder of a helpless indentured servant. But he was crushed to death, slowly and agonizingly, for no convicted crime.

* * * *

Corey was not the only person to escape conviction, although two men—Philip English and John Alden—did not have to go to quite such extremes to avoid the hangman's noose.

Alden and English were about as different as could be. English was unpopular because, despite his name, his family was French. With the French backing the Native Americans during the recent wars in the colonies, this made him a subject of serious suspicion from the start. He had married Mary Hollingsworth, the daughter of a rich merchant, which, together with his successful trading company, meant that he and Mary had more than enough to go around. Both of them were accused as witches and examined in April and May 1692, but due to their wealth and social status, they were not thrown in jail. Instead, when Sheriff Corwin came to their home to arrest Mary one Saturday night, Mary didn't even go with him—she told him to come back the next morning once she'd had a leisurely breakfast. Corwin did so, eager to get his hands on the English fortune. Mary and Philip were then sent to a jail in Boston, but they didn't have to be there all the time. They only slept there; during the day, they were free to move around the town as they pleased.

Until the day of their trial came. That day, Mary and Philip left Boston with the help of a local minister and friend. They fled to New York, only to return once the trials had finally ended the next year.

Alden, on the other hand, was a captain in the army. His father had been one of the Pilgrims that first arrived at Plymouth aboard the *Mayflower*, and Alden seemed to have shared his pioneering spirit. A soldier, sailor, and father of fourteen, Alden was made a target because of rumors that he was supplying enemies—the French-backed Abenaki tribe—with weapons to line his own pockets. This would have been particularly bitter for Mercy Lewis, considering her parents died in Native American raids. She was his main accuser, and Alden viewed his examination with extreme disdain. In his personal account of the trials, he described the accusing girls as "wenches" who "played juggling tricks," clearly considering that their symptoms were completely fake. He was jailed in Boston for almost four months before a group of friends broke him out in mid-September. Like the English couple, Alden fled to New York, where he hid out, ignoring all attempts to get him to stand trial until he was finally cleared by proclamation in 1693.

Chapter 14 – Eight Innocent Firebrands

Three days after Giles Corey suffered the most abominable death, his wife was led to the gallows.

Martha Corey had been sentenced based almost completely on spectral evidence. When she stood trial on September 9th, the accused girls told the jury that they saw the specter of a yellow bird—thought to be Martha's familiar—"sucking" on her hand as she stood in the courtroom. This was the only evidence that Stoughton needed. He was determined to get some kind of plea out of Martha. She was sharp-tongued and opinionated, and she angrily pleaded not guilty, telling the girls that they were lying and loudly denying her belief in witchcraft at all. The jury found her guilty, and she was sentenced to hang on September 22nd, 1692.

By the time that she was sentenced, Giles had, for some time, been protesting that his wife was innocent. She liked to nag, she had a sharp manner, and he didn't like her very much, but he didn't think she was an actual witch—and this may have contributed to his accusation and arrest. In the end, though, Martha outlived Giles by a few days. She knew that her husband had been crushed to death, and perhaps the noose seemed to be merciful in comparison.

But the noose was not merciful. Nothing was merciful about those gallows. Nothing was merciful about the fact that eight innocent people were walking their final walk. Martha was tired, angry, and bitter. Reverend Parris and other members of the church had visited her in jail to officially excommunicate her, and she'd screamed at them to get away from her. How could they do this to her? They had condoned the slow and dreadful torture of her husband, after all. It is perhaps ironic that Giles and Martha may never have been as close or felt as much emotion toward one another as in the days before they both died.

Mary Eastey was also one of the people walking up the hill to be hanged. Perhaps she wept quietly, convinced of her own innocence, her sweet voice unheard by the bloodthirsty crowd. Did the villagers gather with even more enthusiasm than before, ready to see something dramatic as they had at Burroughs' hanging? Or were they growing weary of the wild spectacle of death by now?

The other six people sentenced to die that day were Alice Parker, Wilmot Redd, Samuel Wardwell Sr., Ann Pudeator, Margaret Scott, and Mary Parker. They were all guilty of various small offenses, things that in the eyes of the Putnam family or others among the accusers were utterly unpardonable. Alice Parker, an elderly married lady, was living in a rented house owned by Mary English and could have possibly also been the daughter of Giles Corey. Wilmot Redd, known as "Mammy" to the local fishermen who were colleagues of her husband, made butter for a living and was a crotchety old bat who wasn't popular among the other women. Samuel Wardwell was a carpenter and farmer who had confessed to witchcraft previously but recanted his confession at the last minute and now found himself about to hang for the crime. Ann Pudeator was a well-off widow and known for drinking a bit too much, and she had been employed by Jacob Pudeator as a midwife; when Jacob's wife had passed away, she had promptly married Jacob, which led to accusations that she had killed the late wife with witchcraft. Margaret Scott was an elderly widow who had lost four out of her seven children in their infancy—to witchcraft, her accusers said. And Mary Parker was a nobody, a middle-aged widow whose only crime was sharing the same name with another widow from Andover whose late husband and son had both been mentally unstable.

Cotton Mather would later write of September 22nd, 1692, the deadliest day of the Salem witch trials, that Nicholas Noyes had said out loud "what a sad thing it was to see eight firebrands of Hell hanging there." But the people that died that day were just eight rather ordinary people. Some widows, some married, some women, one a man, each with a story, each with a past, and each with a death sentence. There they all hung, their eyes glazed and staring, ropes creaking as their bodies swung in the fall breeze.

Their deaths brought the Salem death toll up to nineteen hanged, two dead in prison, and one tortured to death. More than 200 people had been accused, and even those who lived would never have their old lives back again, not after the trauma of being betrayed and ostracized by their fellow villagers. Who knows how much longer the hangings would have continued with the many witches still awaiting trial in the jails of Boston and Salem. But someone was about to step in, a dubious hero who was nineteen hangings too late.

Chapter 15 – Glimmers of Sense

The mass hanging of eight people on September 22nd, 1692, almost had an even higher death toll.

Dorcas Hoar, an aged widow from the nearby village of Beverly, Massachusetts, had an entire slew of accusers. It was Thomas Putnam, as usual, and Jonathan Walcott that first filed complaints against her; she was supposed to have afflicted no less than six of the girls. She was arrested on April 30th but would only stand trial on September 6th. This gave her four long months to suffer in imprisonment in Salem.

During those months, at some point, Dorcas decided that it was preferable to confess to a crime she did not commit than to hang for it. When a young man by the name of John Lovett III—visiting his grandmother in jail, who had also been accused as a witch—came by, Dorcas beckoned him nearer to her cell. Lovett presumably knew the old lady, and having compassion on her exhausted and pathetic appearance, he listened as she gave him a tired confession. She told him that she had, indeed, afflicted the girls with witchcraft.

At Dorcas' trial on September 6th, a slew of witnesses testified about the girls' affliction. These included Thomas and Edward Putnam, Joseph Tuck, Mary Gage, Joseph Morgan, Rev. John Hale, and more. Some of the complaints brought against Dorcas were decades old and included fortune-telling and killing animals by witchcraft as well as the affliction of the girls. Lovett, too, testified with regards to Dorcas' confession. She was sentenced to hang, and her execution date was likely set for September 22nd alongside Martha Corey, Mary Eastey, and the six others.

Rev. John Hale had testified during Dorcas' trial that, among other things, Dorcas had stolen out of his house; when his daughter Rebecca came upon Dorcas stealing, the older woman had told her that if she told her father, Dorcas would curse her with witchcraft. That had been fourteen years ago, but it was all evidence against Dorcas now. When he heard Lovett's testimony about Dorcas' confession, however, Hale felt that the old lady might be willing to repent. As a minister, he believed that even though Dorcas was a convicted witch and her life was worth nothing, her soul might yet be saved. If she confessed and repented of witchcraft, she would still have a chance to go to heaven. Because of his belief in this, Hale went to some of the other ministers who were present—Nicholas Noyes among them—and together they wrote a petition to Governor Phips asking for a stay of execution to allow Dorcas time to repent. "Beeing in grat distress of Conscience [she] earnestly craves a little longer time of life to realize & perfect her repentance for the salvation of her soule," the ministers wrote. The petition was sent to Governor Phips, and the ministers' request was granted. Dorcas' execution was postponed.

She was not the only person to be granted a stay of execution. Two other women—Elizabeth Proctor (John Proctor's wife) and Abigail Faulkner Sr.—were given a stay of execution because they were pregnant, allowing them to bear their babies, not that pregnancy or labor in jail could have been at all pleasant.

At first, Dorcas was supposed to have been given just a month to live. But things were changing in Salem. The delusion was starting to fade, and one by one, the people were starting to awaken to what had really taken place among them.

* * * *

Despite the fact that his son Cotton Mather was a loud advocate for the witch trials—having prevented the assembled crowd from uprising after the execution of George Burroughs —Reverend Increase Mather was not at all sure about the trials.

A born Bostonian, Increase had studied in Ireland but soon returned to Massachusetts to become the preacher in the Second Church. By 1674, he was elected as a fellow of Harvard University, and after faithfully serving for more than a decade, he became the president. He had been instrumental in establishing the new Massachusetts Charter, the one that had brought Governor Phips to power, as well as being a personal friend and mentor to Phips. Both Increase and Phips had been in England for some time to petition for the charter, and shortly after their return to Boston and Phips' establishment of the Court of Oyer and Terminer, the governor had been distracted by something even deadlier than the witch trials in Salem: heavy fighting against the French and Native Americans in Maine. Phips had no choice but to leave Boston once again, this time for the front lines.

Despite being described as a conservative Puritan, Increase had been watching the events in Salem unfold from the safety of Boston with rising concern. He knew that Cotton was greatly in favor of the trials, but it was not so easy for Increase to stomach the rising death toll. When Cotton finished his manuscript about the events so far at Salem—misleadingly titled *Wonders of the Invisible World*—Increase was the first to read it. He was horrified at the number of people who were being executed simply on the word of the afflicted. Despite the fact that Increase had actually witnessed and even supported the execution of Burroughs, he was now appalled by the amount of spectral evidence that was being used to kill people. Knowing that the justice system in Salem had apparently dissolved into insanity, Increase had to appeal to someone higher up in the food chain. He wrote directly to his friend, Governor Phips.

When Phips returned from the war in Maine during October 1692, he found Salem and Boston in absolute chaos. He was horrified to discover that his Court of Oyer and Terminer had been hanging people left, right, and center based on spectral evidence. Worse still, Phips discovered that his own wife, Mary Phips, had been accused of witchcraft.

Phips may have established the court that had sentenced nineteen people to hang and tortured one to death, but he may not have expected it to be quite so zealous in its persecution of the so-called witches. Shortly after his arrival back in Boston, he wrote to the king and queen back in England that as soon as he returned to Massachusetts, he had suspended the Court of Oyer and Terminer. He had also prohibited any more arrests and completely barred the use of spectral evidence, and the eight children who were still in custody were all released on bail. Dorothy Good, tragically, was not one of them. Her father was still trying to scrape together the money to set her free; Dorothy would only leave the jail on December 10th after nine months of imprisonment. She was never the same again.

At least, little Dorothy would never have to hang. A voice of sense had spoken at last, and this time, the voice was loud and powerful enough to put a stop to the madness. There were no more executions after Phips returned. But the trouble was by no means over yet; Phips was still faced with a vast number of people filling up the jails of Salem and Boston, waiting to be tried. Tragically, some of those people would wait six more months before they could see the light of day.

And some, even though proven innocent, would never be free again.

Chapter 16 – Not Guilty

The Court of Oyer and Terminer had been dissolved on October 29th at Phips' order, one month and seven days after the mass hanging of eight people. However, with more than fifty cases still waiting to be heard, Phips still had to establish some system to get them out of jail and close the cases. His solution was a Superior Court of Judicature, and once again, he put Stoughton in charge of it.

Stoughton was only nineteen years old when he graduated from Harvard with a degree in theology. He worked as a preacher for many years until the new charter, and Phips with it, gave him the job as Chief Justice of Massachusetts—a questionable decision considering that Stoughton had absolutely no legal qualifications. Uneducated in the law and bringing with him a strongly conservative Puritan bias, Stoughton was part of the reason why the madness in Salem was allowed to continue for so long.

It is not known why Phips would choose to allow Stoughton to continue leading the proceedings. This time, though, at least the governor was going to be sure of one thing: he was going to keep the Chief Justice on a very short leash.

* * * *

The first trial of the Salem witch hunt in which absolutely no spectral evidence would be allowed began on January 4th, 1693.

The act that established the Superior Court of Judicature had only been passed on December 16th. By this time, some of the accused had been in jail for eight months or longer, awaiting their trial. Although this was at least moderately better than being hanged for no crime, there must have been considerable suffering still. At last, though, a fair chance was being given, and there was a glimmer of hope for Sarah Buckley and her daughter, Mary Witheridge.

Hope was not something that Sarah and Mary were well acquainted with. When Sarah had first married William Buckley, he had owned a modest piece of land and had some skills as a cobbler. She had expected to live an ordinary, happy, free life in the New World, where her parents had brought her as a little girl. Sarah and William had produced eight children and settled into a comfortable life until the day that William lost a lawsuit against the former governor of Massachusetts. All his land was seized, and shortly afterward, he lost all of his cobblers' tools in repaying a debt incurred by one of their sons.

William's misfortune left him and Sarah completely destitute, not unlike the Good family. They had no way of earning an income and nowhere to go. Sarah's daughter, Mary, was not faring any better, as she had become a widow. Their luck took a turn for the worse in 1692 when they were both accused of witchcraft, their poverty and status as outsiders making them ideal targets. They were arrested on the same day in May and had been awaiting trial for seven long months.

Now, they were brought at last before the Superior Court to hear their fates. Sarah had two hopes to cling to: the first was the banishment of spectral evidence, and the second was a minister from the neighboring village of Ipswich had written a testimony to her good character. The trial was swift, and it was bitter for Stoughton because, without spectral evidence, there was simply no reason for either Sarah or Mary to be accused with anything at all. The afflicted girls could only watch, their fits worth nothing now, their wild testimonies utterly useless, as the women that they hated were told that they could go free. Sarah Buckley and Mary Witheridge, along with two other women, were the first people to be found not guilty during the Salem witch trials.

They were allowed to return to their lives, and even though they were impoverished, at least they were free. Paying for their board for the time they had spent in jail stripped the very last of their possessions from them, and after that, Sarah simply disappears from history. Mary, however, married Benjamin Proctor—a fellow accused witch who was also set free by the Superior Court of Judicature. He had lost his father, John Proctor, to one of the hangings. His mother, Elizabeth, by virtue of her pregnancy, had been sentenced to death but was pardoned in 1693. And so, after more than half a year in jail for no good reason, the real victims of the Salem witch trials began to pick up the pieces and to put their lives back together, despite the best efforts of those who would watch them suffer.

* * * *

By January 10th, less than a week after the first session of the Supreme Court of Judicature, the names of eleven people had been cleared. Hope and normality were beginning to return to the lives of the accused, and for those still in jail awaiting trial, there was a light at the end of the long tunnel of their awful imprisonment. These people had gone to jail believing that, no matter how innocent they were, they faced one of two choices: confess to a crime they did not commit and then live with that stigma against them or accept the death sentence. But with every person who was set free, those still waiting in jail grew in hope. There was no doubt that their lives would be very different if they were freed, considering that in that time, it was required for all prisoners to pay for their imprisonment once they were set free, regardless of whether or not they had been proven innocent. But at least there was hope for freedom.

Yet not all of the accused were found to be not guilty. Sarah Wardwell was the first to be found guilty by the Superior Court of

Judicature. The wife of Samuel Wardwell, who had been hanged on September 22nd alongside seven others, she had been married twice. Her first husband, Adam Hawkes, was an old man for whom Sarah had no attraction and no desire to marry; however, she was pressured into the union, as he was very rich. They had one child together—a little girl—before Hawkes died and left Sarah a considerable fortune, making her young, wealthy, and ridiculously eligible. She was courted constantly by a variety of suitors who were chasing her money, but instead, she married Samuel Wardwell, despite the fact that he had not had a penny to his name. This would lead some to speculate that Samuel had bewitched her into marrying him.

During her interrogation on September 1st, Sarah confessed to being a witch. She was still in jail three weeks later when Samuel was hanged but had not yet stood trial when Phips dissolved the Court of Oyer and Terminer. Her detailed confession at the Superior Court of Judicature meant that the jury had little choice other than to find her guilty on January 10th. She was sentenced to death.

The very next day, the court condemned its second defendant to die, Elizabeth Johnson Jr. And again, on January 12th, Mary Post was found guilty. While several other so-called witches were cleared in those three days—Sarah Wardwell's daughters, Sarah Hawkes and Mercy Wardwell, Mary Bridges Sr., Hannah Post, Sarah Bridges, and Mary Osgood were all found not guilty; Mary Black and Thomas Farrar Sr. were cleared by proclamation—the fact that the Superior Court of Judicature was still willing to execute witches was worrying.

But Salem had seen enough hangings, and Governor Phips had had enough of the death toll. He wrote pardons for all three of the condemned women. They were all set free, and in trials that went on until the middle of May 1693, all of the accused were found not guilty.

Chapter 17 – The Last Casualty

Lydia Dustin had been a widow for twenty years.

Now an elderly woman, Lydia had lost her husband Josiah when she was in her late forties. They had lived a prosperous life together, having had several children—little is known of Lydia's life prior to the witch trials, but they definitely had at least two daughters. Even after Josiah's death, Lydia was able to get by, as he had owned large amounts of land in the nearby town of Redding. She was known as a fairly wealthy and popular lady in the area, and Josiah had been a leader in the community. But no amount of wealth or popularity had been able to save people like Rebecca Nurse or Philip and Mary English from the accusations. Lydia was arrested on April 30th based on accusations by Mercy Lewis, Abigail Williams, Ann Putnam Jr., and Mary Walcott. George Burroughs, Philip English, and Dorcas Hoar were some of the others whose arrest warrants went out that day.

Unlike Burroughs and Hoar, however, Lydia's trial was for some reason postponed at great length. The Court of Oyer and Terminer would try many people in the following five months before it was dissolved, but Lydia was not one of them. She waited in jail, not knowing what was going to happen to her or to her two daughters, Sarah Dustin and Mary Colson. Both of them had been arrested and were also awaiting trial. At least Mary's daughter, Elizabeth Colson, had evaded arrest; she was in hiding now, and Lydia hoped that she would stay that way.

The dissolution of the Court of Oyer and Terminer was a glimmer of hope for Lydia and her daughters, and when the news started to come in about how many people the new Superior Court of Judicature were finding not guilty, the women started to feel some hope and optimism for the first time in months. However, there was still a long wait ahead of them. By the time the Superior Court of Judicature was finally ready to start trials, Lydia had been in jail for eight long months, and the conditions there were starting to take their toll on her aging body. Sickness was rampant in Boston's jail, crammed full as it was by witchcraft suspects; the food was poor, the cells were cold, and it was no place for the elderly to spend a night in, let along eight long months. Lydia was fading fast right before the eyes of her two daughters.

Lydia and Sarah Dustin were both to be tried on the same day. Staggering with weakness, Lydia made her way to the courtroom on February 1st, 1693; she had been in jail for almost exactly nine months. She was old and shaky at this point, but she was determined to see her daughters cleared, and cleared they were. Sarah Dustin, Mary Colson, and Lydia Dustin were all found not guilty.

This was cause for great rejoicing, but Lydia would soon find out that freedom was not that simple. Thanks to the greedy Sheriff Corwin, the fortune that Josiah had left his loving wife when he died in 1671 was all gone; it had been seized by the state while Lydia was in jail. Sarah was unmarried and had no income of her own. Both of them would not be freed until they could pay off their board from the many months that they had been imprisoned. The injustice of it must have been utterly appalling. Lydia and Sarah had been proven to be not guilty of any offense whatsoever, yet they had served nine months in jail despite their innocence. In a modern justice system, they would be the ones who were owed money for the months of their life that had been taken from them. Instead, destitute, penniless, and aged, Lydia found herself with no way out. Neither she nor

Sarah could pay their board. They were cleared, but they were not released, and they were sent back to live behind bars.

For six long weeks, Lydia clung to life, or what was left of her life now that she was still trapped in a Bostonian jail despite her innocence. But on March 10th, 1693—almost five months after the last mass hanging of the Salem witch trials—Lydia succumbed at last to old age and illness. She may not have been sentenced to die, but she was killed by the Salem witch trials as surely as those tragic victims who had been hanged on Gallows Hill, just like the others that died in prison. She goes down in history as the last casualty.

* * * *

Two months after Lydia's death, on May 11th, 1693, the last man still awaiting trial—William Hobbs—was cleared by proclamation. An end had come at last to the madness of Salem, and a semblance of normality began to return to the village, but there was no wiping away the ugly stain that the trials had left on its history.

Chapter 18 – Life After the Trials

The underbearers of Sheriff George Corwin's coffin were not particularly sober. As with any funeral, Corwin's had been preceded by a gathering the previous night, and the young men who carried his coffin had helped themselves to a considerable amount of liquor. To give themselves a little strength and courage for the long task of carrying his coffin all the way from the site of the funeral service to the communal burying ground some distance away, they had decided to drink a little more and were now somewhat unsteadily moving through the verdant green morning in the spring of April 1696.

Corwin had lived for only three years after the end of the witch trials, but they had been three years of great abundance. He might not have been able to torture Giles Corey into a confession, meaning that his estate remained just out of Corwin's grasp, but there had been plenty of other rich victims and plenty of loot for a greedy sheriff with sticky fingers. Corwin was in charge of handling the confiscated wealth, and instead of paying the due monies to the British Crown, he had a reputation for sneaking it into his own pocket. And no estate had proven more lucrative than what he had managed to seize from Philip and Mary English. The wealthy couple may have succeeded in escaping their jail sentence, but Corwin had promptly pillaged their extensive property while they were hiding out in New York, and the Englishes had returned to find their home and lands stripped almost bare.

Even after the trials, Philip had been petitioning the Crown to pay him back, but his efforts had been unsuccessful considering that the Crown itself had seen precious little of the money and property that Corwin had taken. Philip knew that Corwin was behind this. He was, by 1696, an angry and embittered man; Mary had died in childbirth shortly after their return to Massachusetts, and Philip had nothing left but his wealth. He couldn't bear the fact that Corwin had died and gotten away with it.

Or had he?

The underbearers wandered on, bearing Corwin's coffin on their shoulders with as much decorum as they could manage in their somewhat intoxicated state. It was still far more decorum than had been afforded to Giles Corey when the rocks were pushed off his shattered body and he was tossed ignominiously into an unmarked grave. The thick foliage of the woods they were walking through filtered the warm sunshine, making it pale green and welcome on their skin.

Then the bushes erupted. Armed men charged forth from their cover, and the panicking underbearers found themselves surrounded by a group of soldiers. Among them, a dashing young man on a fine horse rode up to the underbearers and told them brusquely that he would be taking Corwin's coffin. The men were in no shape to defend themselves or their dead acquaintance. They dumped the coffin and fled as Philip English triumphantly rode off with the body of his nemesis. He refused to give it back to Corwin's family until he was paid everything that Corwin had taken from him, and in due course, over 500 pounds sterling—around $100,000 in today's money—was paid back to him. True to his word, Philip then gave the somewhat decomposed Corwin back to his family, and he could be buried at last.

* * * *

The responses of those who had been involved in the witch trials were as many and varied as the individuals themselves.

The afflicted girls, who had become so famous overnight, found themselves stripped of all of their status and credibility when Phips banned the use of spectral evidence. One can only imagine what it must have been like to move forward afterward. Some of the girls, like nine-year-old Betty Parris, had been so young when they had made their accusations that they barely understood what they were saying—or what they had done to those who were convicted. Little Betty would someday grow old enough to realize that her testimony had taken innocent lives. Or perhaps, if she had genuinely been sick and hallucinating instead of simply lying, she would grow up still believing that some of the people who had so cruelly afflicted her had gone free and might strike back at her again at any moment. Either way, we can only speculate that Betty had condemned herself to a lifetime of either guilt or anxiety. She did, however, succeed in living a full and free life afterward; she married Benjamin Barron in 1710 and raised four children before her death at a ripe old age of 78 in 1760. This was a lot more than many of the people she had accused ever got to experience. While Betty had four children, Sarah Good, hanged for witchcraft on Betty's accusation, would never get to see her two little girls grow up; Mercy died in her arms due to the conditions in jail, and Dorothy would live in a tragic state of mental illness for the rest of her life.

Betty's father, Samuel, was astoundingly allowed to remain a minister of Salem for another four years after the trials ended. Despite the fact that many of his sermons had fueled the rising tide of accusations, no legal action was ever taken against him, although a group of dissenters did voice their disgust for his behavior in February 1693 by withdrawing from the church. Many of the dissenters were family of the accused that had died (including Samuel Nurse, the son of Rebecca Nurse and cousin of Mary Eastey), but their voices were not heard, and Reverend Parris was allowed to continue. In the end, it was not his involvement in the witch trials that would get him thrown out of Salem, but the arguments over his salary and the ownership of the parsonage that had been going on since he was first ordained. He left Salem, by now a widower, and settled in Sudbury, Massachusetts. Appallingly, he would continue to preach there for the rest of his working life. He died in 1720.

Abigail "Nabby" Williams, also one of the first accusers, simply vanished from history. She would likely have left Salem with Betty and Samuel Parris, but there is no further record about her after her last testimony on June 3rd, 1692.

Elizabeth Hubbard's life after the trials is similarly obscured; she may have moved away from Salem, gotten married, and had four children just like Betty, but this is not certain. Considering that Elizabeth may have started her accusations as a result of her uncertainty over ever finding a suitor, this would be intensely ironic.

One of the most damaging accusers of them all, Ann Putnam Jr., would be the only one of all the girls involved who would later publicly apologize for her actions. Ann, at least, was the one girl who felt guilt instead of fear. She was only twelve years old and strongly influenced by her family's rivalry with the Proctors and other families in the area, and she was likely being persuaded or forced into making her accusations by her mother, Ann Putnam Sr. In 1706, now 26 years old, orphaned, and capable of making her own choices, Ann recognized that the whole thing had been either a hallucination or a horrible falsehood spurred on by her mother's ulterior motives. Her apology was read in church with her present, and she expressed regret at her actions, blaming them on a "great delusion of Satan" and saying that none of these actions were as a result of malice. Considering that she accused 62 people of witchcraft, the burden on her conscience must have been tremendous, and she seems to have lived the rest of her life trying desperately to make up for it. Both of her parents—likely the real accusers and those truly responsible for Ann's testimonies—died when she was only nineteen, and Ann would remain single for the rest of her life, devoted to raising her nine younger siblings, one of whom was just an infant when they were all orphaned. It appears to have taken a great toll on her; only ten years after her apology, she died a young spinster.

Even some of the judges who had written the death sentences for the accused seemed to have felt some remorse. One of them, Samuel Sewall, publicly apologized after the trials. John Hathorne, however, seemed to feel no such guilt; even though he would flatly accuse defendants like Bridget Bishop of lying when their testimonies did not agree with those of the accusers, he lived in Salem and worked as a judge for many more years before dying in 1717. His great-great-grandson would grow up to become the novelist and writer Nathaniel Hawthorne, who detested his ancestor so much that he changed his surname from Hathorne to Hawthorne just to distance himself from the hated judge.

William Stoughton, who had been in charge of most of the trials, would continue to climb the political ranks, even working as the acting governor for six years after Phips died in London in 1695. Stoughton, Massachusetts, is named after him.

As for the victims, even those who had been released and returned to their lives could never be the same again. Most of them would have become completely destitute, having had to pay for their board. Many also lost family members in the executions, considering that it was common for more than one person in a family to be arrested and accused of witchcraft. Elizabeth Proctor was one of them; she had lost her husband, John, to one of the mass hangings. She had always denied her involvement in witchcraft, saying, "I take God in heaven to be my witness, that I know nothing of it, no more than the child unborn." That child unborn was the only reason why Elizabeth had escaped the noose, as she had been given a stay of execution because of her pregnancy. Despite the best efforts of friends and family members who petitioned for both Proctors to be released, John was hanged, and Elizabeth was sentenced to die as soon as her baby was old enough.

She was still in jail awaiting trial when she gave birth to the little one: a son, whom she named after his deceased father. Baby John was almost three months old, and he and his mother were still living in jail when a group of people, including Elizabeth's stepsons, petitioned again for her release. Again, the petition was not granted. She would only be released in May 1693 after her family had paid her board, a necessity because Elizabeth had no money; John had not left her anything in the will he composed in jail because she was sentenced to death, leaving everything to their children instead. Her stepson Benjamin, who had petitioned for her release, took her and baby John in to live with him and Mary Witheridge, whom he had married. She and her children stayed with Benjamin and Mary until Elizabeth remarried in 1699.

Deliverance Hobbs, who had confessed to witchcraft and implicated several others including Sarah Osborne, George Burroughs, and her own husband William, was allowed to go free because of her confession. However, William had never stopped professing his innocence. He escaped from jail in 1692 and abandoned Deliverance and his daughter, Abigail, both of whom had told the court that he was a witch. He was the last of the accused to be cleared by proclamation. Deliverance's confession saved her from the noose, but it bought her a lifetime of loneliness and bitterness.

Tituba's confession had similarly spared her life, but she was stuck in prison for months. Because she belonged to Samuel Parris, he was supposedly responsible for paying her board and getting her out of jail. Of course, Parris had no interest in doing this, and she was only freed when he sold her and her husband to another person—it is uncertain who this buyer was—and she and John Indian were both moved out of Salem. Tituba simply disappears from history at this point, and it is unknown what happened to her after the trials. Tituba had never been free, and since it would be almost 200 years before the abolition of slavery in North America, she probably never lived any part of her life in freedom.

Chapter 19 – The Second Salem

Two hundred years had passed for Salem, and the witch trials had faded into an ugly part of history. The town had grown, adding a great wharf, Fort Lee, and a library. It had raised its drawbridge in 1775 to keep the British out during the American Revolution, built the ship *Friendship of Salem*, and been the setting for Nathaniel Hawthorne's birth and also his novel *The House of Seven Gables*. The religious face of the village had changed, too. It was no longer the purely Puritan colony that it once had been. As early as 1805, the First Universalist Congregation made their home in the village, which had by now grown into a town. Universalism was almost the total opposite of Puritanism; Christian Universalism was founded on the basis that no human soul would ever end up in hell, quite the contrast with Puritanism's constant vigilance for souls that had already allied themselves to the devil. And it was a movement not unlike Universalism that would give rise to the last witchcraft trial in American history.

Mary Baker Eddy, born Mary Baker in Bow, New Hampshire, had had a difficult childhood. Raised by a strict, stern, hot-tempered Protestant Congregationalist father who had also been a Justice of the Peace, she was just as strong-willed as he was, and they clashed frequently. His subsequent abuse of the girl led to a myriad of problems. She suffered from frequent "fits"—which may have been seizures, fainting as a result of poor nutrition, or simply hysteria—

and her father's angry attitude about these fits eventually led her to succumb to an eating disorder that all but starved her. She was sickly and kept out of school because she had been diagnosed with "a brain too big for her head." Even her first marriage could not save her; despite the fact that Mary appeared to have been quite happy with George Washington Glover, she lost him only months after they were married when she was six months pregnant with her first child.

It was during her widowhood that Mary began to write articles for publications that were involved in much more liberal thinking than that to which she had been exposed during her strict Protestant childhood, supporting fraternities such as the Freemasons. Her health, however, continued to decline to such an extent that she had to give up her little boy when he was only four years old, and her second husband refused to take custody of him; she would only hear from the boy again when he was a grown man. She didn't have much luck with her new husband, either. After more than a decade, he walked out on her.

Even Mary's third husband, Asa Eddy, didn't last—dead after a few years of marriage—but by this point, she had delved into something else, something that she believed would give her the answers to everything. In fact, she plunged into the development of a whole new religion. Her book, *Science and Health*, put forth her argument that there was no such thing as disease—it was simply a delusion, incurable by medicine, and could only be removed by prayer. The book was published in 1875; by 1879, her theology had gained such a tremendous following that it had become a separate denomination of Christianity known as Christian Science. She built the First Church of Christ, Scientist in Boston in 1894.

Before Christian Science was formally recognized as a denomination, however, it was an academy. Established in an old building on Broad Street, Lynn, Massachusetts, the Mary B. Glover's Christian Scientists' Home took in anyone who wanted to be educated on how to become a "doctor" of Christian Science. One of these was Daniel Spofford, a young man who fell head over heels in love with Eddy's charisma and character. He hung on her every word as she taught him all about how to heal diseases only with his hands and his mind, especially expounding on the theory of animal magnetism. This theory had been developed by Franz Anton Mesmer in the late 18th century but had gained popularity and was quickly melding with Christian Science. Mesmer had believed that there was a mysterious fluid, called animal magnetism, that flowed through all living bodies. Disease of any kind, Mesmer wrote, was caused by a clot or blockage in the flow of this fluid. And all disease could be healed by manipulating the magnetic poles of the body. Eddy was quick to jump onto this theory and mix it in with Christian Science, ending up training her doctors in this mesmerism in order to heal others, but she did believe that it could also be used for evil, in which case she called it malicious animal magnetism.

Spofford lapped it all up, becoming one of her most devoted students, and it came to the point where Eddy once hinted that she might choose him as her successor to lead Christian Science. Spofford was delighted; so delighted, in fact, that he left his wife, hoping that Eddy was as charmed by him as he was by her. Sadly, for Spofford, Eddy had no such designs for him, and when they argued over money in 1877, she spurned all of his advances and even threw him out of the Christian Scientists' Home.

Angered though he was by Eddy's behavior, Spofford continued to "practice" his mesmerism as a healer. One of his patients was Lucretia Brown, an old lady with a variety of health issues, including a spinal injury that had left her bedridden. She sought help originally from a different doctor of mesmerism, and she had experienced such an improvement that she continued to seek visits from mesmerists to aid her healing. One of these mesmerists turned out to be Spofford, and when Lucretia suffered a terrible relapse that landed her back in bed after a few months of glorious freedom, she decided that Spofford was the culprit. She asked Eddy to represent her interests, and the hot-tempered leader of Christian Science was all too happy to pursue the case. She had Spofford brought up against the Supreme

Judicial Court in none other than Salem, Massachusetts, in May 1878 on charges of witchcraft.

Perhaps Eddy had hoped that she would get the same results as the accusers in the same town had almost 200 years ago. Perhaps she fantasized about Spofford hanging by his neck on Gallows Hill, his face purple, his eyes lifeless. But it was not 1692 anymore, and the judges were not Hathorne or Stoughton; instead, it was the end of the 19th century, and Judge Horace Gray had no time for such drama. A born Bostonian and educated at Harvard, Gray was deeply familiar with the witchcraft trials of 1692, and he was in no mind to watch history repeat itself; he was also intensely conservative and stuck religiously to precedent. Despite the fact that Eddy showed up with a whole crowd of supporters and witnesses, her case was promptly dismissed.

Chapter 20 – Remembering Salem

Illustration V: A memorial to Elizabeth Howe quotes her words at her trial in Salem Memorial Park, Salem, Massachusetts

Tim1965, CC BY 3.0 https://creativecommons.org/licenses/by/3.0 via Wikimedia Commons https://commons.wikimedia.org/wiki/File:Salem_innocence.jpg

Over the decades that followed the Salem Witch Trials, the General Court began to realize more and more what a horrific and tragic mistake had been made by the justice system in Salem. As early as 1697, a fast day was declared in Massachusetts in remembrance of Salem's victims; it was on that day that Samuel Sewall published his apology, alongside the jury foreman from the trials and eleven of his jurors. "[We] do therefore humbly beg for forgiveness," they wrote. "We would none of us do such things again on such grounds for the whole world."

In the same year, Reverend John Hale—the leader of the group who had petitioned for Dorcas Hoar's stay of execution and thus ended up saving her life—published a book denouncing the trials and the behavior of witnesses, jurors, magistrates, and accusers, including himself. Robert Calef, who had witnessed the trials in Salem as well as the hanging of his friend Ann Glover in Boston in 1688, had also published an account entitled *More Wonders of the Invisible World* to counter Cotton Mather's publication of a similar name.

During the beginning of the 18th century, realizing that the state had come to deeply regret its actions, the families of the victims felt that they had a voice at last. They started to petition the government to fix what it had broken—to clear the names of all those who had been executed and pay their families reparations for the tragedy. Victims who had been imprisoned but who were found not guilty also started to demand that the government should pay them back for money or property that they had lost during their imprisonment thanks to the likes of Sheriff Corwin—although these victims didn't quite take as radical an approach as Philip English had.

Joseph Green, Parris' successor as minister of Salem, had a lot of rebuilding to do. The church building itself may have stood just as tall and proud as ever, but its people were torn apart by conflict, shattered by guilt and fear, and uncertain of what they could believe. Green had the unenviable task of attempting to make some kind of meaning out of the chaos within the context of Puritanism, and he appears to have done his best to go about it. Forgiveness was a core theme in his sermons; in fact, he went as far as changing the seating in the church itself during sermons, making former enemies sit next to each other as if they were friends. The Putnams and Proctors found themselves side by side, and Green sought for reconciliation and healing, perhaps proving himself to be one of the few contemporary people of Salem who recognized the real enemy.

By 1712, Green had also taken an enormous step toward peace of mind and healing for the families of the victims of the trials when he reversed the excommunications of Rebecca Nurse and Martha and Giles Corey. Their families may have been mourning twice over for their loved ones, believing that because of their excommunication, the unjustly executed would burn in hell instead of going to heaven, despite their faith. Green's reversal of the excommunication was a powerful symbol to them.

As the 18th century fell away, America and the world changed. Superstition began to fade, leading most Americans to question whether witchcraft even existed in the first place. By the late 19th century, the accused of the Salem witch trials were no longer seen as criminals at all; in fact, it had become obvious that they were the true victims, not the "afflicted" girls who had accused them.

Today, all of the victims of the trials have been given a reversal of attainder, clearing their names posthumously; ridiculously, the last victims were only cleared in 2001 by the signing of a resolution by Governor of Massachusetts Jane Swift. Various memorials to the victims are also peppered throughout Salem (previously Salem Town) and Danvers (previously Salem Village). Salem Memorial Park was opened in 1992 on the 300th anniversary of the trials; the names of all the victims are etched into the park's wall. A memorial to Rebecca Nurse was erected in 1885, alongside another memorial to the neighbors and friends who had tried to save her, which was added seven years later.

The story of the Salem witch trials has also been perpetuated in a variety of different mediums in the modern day. One of the most prominent of these, a play named *The Crucible* by Arthur Miller, drew parallels between the events in Salem and the 1950s "witch hunt" of communists in the United States during the Cold War. Its protagonist was John Proctor, casting the "afflicted" girls in the role of antagonist, and it ended with Proctor on the gallows in his final moments. The play was reproduced for opera, film, and television. More recently, the trials have become the inspiration for a variety of mediums in popular culture, among them the horror television series *Salem* (2014), which draws on historical characters.

One question that still remains unanswered and intrigues scientists and historians to this day is exactly what happened and why the trials got so quickly out of hand. Central to this question is what was actually happening to the afflicted girls. One theory is centered on the whole thing being a conspiracy theory caused by manipulative parents or guardians, considering that all of the afflicted girls had ties to the Putnam family in some way or another. In this theory, Samuel Parris and the Putnams got together to make their children behave in a certain way in order to gain power and get back at their enemies, John and Elizabeth Proctor prominent among them.

Another theory, one which seems to hold some weight among the scientific community, is that the girls really were sick—just not with witchcraft. Samuel Parris' salary came one-third in the form of money and two-thirds in the form of provisions, and bread was a staple of their diet, with rye bread being popular. Rye bread, however, is prone to a fungus named *Claviceps purpurea*, from which the drug LSD is derived. When growing in bread, the fungus gives off alkaloids known as ergot. These alkaloids are as hallucinogenic as they are poisonous. Symptoms of the poisoning include seizures, spasms, paresthesia (sensations of the skin that do not appear to have an external cause), and psychosis. This may explain the "contortions," "fits," and feelings of being pinched or pricked that the girls described, and the substance's hallucinogenic properties may explain the specters that they saw. The theory is imperfect—no mention is made of gastrointestinal illness in the testimonies of the girls, which normally proceeds the neurological symptoms of ergot poisoning—but it is supported by the fact that witch hunts were less prevalent in areas where rye was not a popular grain.

The bottom line, sadly, is that we still don't know exactly what happened to cause the Salem witch trials. The girls might have been poisoned, and all of the accusers and their supporters may have genuinely believed that the strange symptoms were evidence of witchcraft, even truly believing that their enemies had caused it as they were the most likely suspects for afflicting the girls. Perhaps the girls and their parents made the whole thing up for selfish reasons. As in other witch trials both before and after Salem, the girls may have come up with everything by themselves, seeking attention in a world that didn't pay much mind to women. Or it could have simply been a combination of all of the above factors. Some modern religious people believe that witchcraft really was involved, but whatever actually happened, everyone can agree that the whole thing got completely out of hand, with innocent deaths as the heartbreaking result. Until science can uncover what history is not clear on, we still won't have a definitive answer.

Conclusion

Selfish people, attention-seeking adolescents, family feuds, moldy bread—Salem's "witchcraft" could have been caused by anything, but the combination of factors would never have come together to form the perfect storm if it wasn't for one thing: the flaws of human nature.

When the trials were still happening, they were focused only on the sin of witchcraft. Reading back through the history, however, the trials don't tell the story of one single type of flaw or mistake. Instead, the story is about the hideous plethora of human vice: fear, guilt, selfish ambition, prejudice, neglect, pride, falsehood. The cast of villains in this story is huge and diverse. They range through a variety of antagonists as scary and powerful as the baddies in any ghost story: opportunistic Elizabeth Hubbard, looking for fame to give herself a future; the frightened Tituba, whose confession killed Sarah Osborne, Sarah Good, and even Sarah's unborn daughter in order to escape the noose herself; harsh and ambitious Samuel Parris, determined to bend the argumentative new parish to his own will; the biased John Hathorne, condemning his victims as guilty before they even walked into the courtroom; cruel and vindictive Ann Putnam Sr., manipulating her sick little daughter in order to advance her personal agenda. And that is to name just a few.

In fact, first diving into the history of these trials is as depressing as it is horrific. Here lies the story of how even pure things—little children and their innocent faith—can be twisted into something awful. How the small and mundane vices of ordinarily nasty people could spiral into the massacre of more than twenty innocent lives. The most terrifying thing about the Salem debacle is the fact that we can find no single, central, appalling antagonist, no evil genius masterminding the chaos, no Darth Vader or Thanos behind the deaths. None of them planned to take over the world or leave a scorch mark on the pages of history. Some of these people were looking to save their own lives, instead condemning others to die as they rambled on in their confessions, hoping to strike a chord in the audience that would help lead to their pardon. These people were guilty of the same everyday evil that we find all around us and even within ourselves: selfishness, pride, greed, malice. And those ordinary vices hanged nineteen people, tortured one to death, and allowed six others to die lingering deaths in jail, as well as to destroy the lives of the other accused who were imprisoned for so long.

With all of its spooky accouterments, the story of Salem is easy to warp into a horror story. But at its heart, it's a cautionary tale. Ordinary people in the United States today are no longer hanging other people for witchcraft, of course. Yet it's still all too easy for the sum of our small vices to be greater than their parts, for our suspicion and bias to run away with us.

And there is still room for a protagonist in this tale. This book is meant not to condemn mankind but to be read in honor of the small handful of courageous heroes and those people who did not deserve to die in such a horrendous manner. Giles Corey, crying, "More weight!" as he died to give his sons their inheritance. The swashbuckling Philip English, spiriting his wife out of danger and refusing to back down for what he knew belonged to him. Increase Mather, going against the popular opinion of his beloved religion to denounce the use of spectral evidence. The faceless and nameless neighbors who petitioned so hard for the release of Rebecca Nurse. And the nineteen men and women who hanged for their crimes when such an easy way out was offered them: to confess, to implicate others, and to go free. They would rather die than live with guilt over a crime that they had not committed.

This is not just the story of the Salem witch trials. This is the story of its victims, and they will never be forgotten.

Here's another book by Captivating History that you might like

Free Bonus from Captivating History (Available for a Limited time)

Hi History Lovers!

Now you have a chance to join our exclusive history list so you can get your first history ebook for free as well as discounts and a potential to get more history books for free! Simply visit the link below to join.

Captivatinghistory.com/ebook

Also, make sure to follow us on Facebook, Twitter and Youtube by searching for Captivating History.

Sources

https://www.irishcentral.com/roots/history/goody-ann-glover-irish-native-last-witch-hanged-boston

https://the-history-blogger.com/2018/08/29/the-irishwoman-hanged-for-witchcraft-ann-goody-glover/

https://salemwitchtrialsresearch.wordpress.com/2015/02/26/goody-glover-the-boston-witch-of-1688/

https://www.thoughtco.com/european-witch-hunts-timeline-3530786

https://www.bbc.com/news/magazine-14490790

https://www.historic-uk.com/CultureUK/The-Pendle-Witches/

https://www.jw.org/en/publications/magazines/g201405/european-witch-hunts/

https://owlcation.com/humanities/Why-Did-the-Puritans-Really-Leave-England-For-The-New-World

https://www.britannica.com/biography/John-Endecott

https://www.creativenorthshore.com/2015/10/19/salems-most-famous-statue-is-not-a-witch/

https://www.thewitchhouse.org/

https://www.salem.org/salem-history/

https://www.legendsofamerica.com/ma-samuelparris/

https://www.encyclopedia.com/social-sciences/social-sciences-magazines/parris-samuel

https://www.thoughtco.com/definition-of-witchs-cake-3528206

https://www.thoughtco.com/abigail-williams-biography-3530316

https://allthatsinteresting.com/abigail-williams

https://historyofmassachusetts.org/betty-parris-first-afflicted-girl-of-the-salem-witch-trials/

https://historyofmassachusetts.org/abigail-williams-salem/

https://salemwitchtrialsresearch.wordpress.com/2015/01/16/doctor-who-griggs-and-the-witch-trials/

http://88617866nhd.weebly.com/the-physician-who-diagnosed-bewitchment.html

http://www.hawthorneinsalem.org/Literature/Quakers&Witches/YoungGoodmanBrown/MMD823.html

https://www.thoughtco.com/tituba-salem-witch-trials-3530572

https://historyofmassachusetts.org/tituba-the-slave-of-salem/

https://www.history.com/news/salem-witch-trials-first-accused-woman-slave

https://historyofmassachusetts.org/john-hathorne-the-salem-witch-judge/

https://www.thoughtco.com/tituba-salem-witch-trials-3530572

http://salem.lib.virginia.edu/people/nursecourt.html

http://www.womenhistoryblog.com/2008/06/martha-and-giles-corey.html

https://historyofmassachusetts.org/martha-corey/

https://historyofmassachusetts.org/mary-warren/

https://www.legendsofamerica.com/ma-salemafflicted/3/

https://www.legendsofamerica.com/ma-salemafflicted/2/#elizabeth-hubbard

https://historicipswich.org/2015/03/24/four-year-old-dorothy-good-is-jailed-for-witchcraft-march-24-1692/

http://salem.lib.virginia.edu/n62.html

https://famous-trials.com/salem/2042-sal-bbur

https://historyofmassachusetts.org/reverend-george-burroughs-salem/

https://www.thoughtco.com/george-burroughs-3529133

http://salem.lib.virginia.edu/n95.html

https://www.thoughtco.com/sarah-good-biography-3530339

https://www.legendsofamerica.com/ma-salemcourt/3/

https://famous-trials.com/salem/2035-sal-bphi

http://people.ucls.uchicago.edu/~snekros/New%20World%20News/New_World_News/Corruption_in_the_Colony.html

http://salem.lib.virginia.edu/people/phips.html

https://www.accessible-archives.com/2015/06/bridget-bishop-hanged-at-salems-gallows-hill/

https://www.history.com/this-day-in-history/first-salem-witch-hanging

https://www.thoughtco.com/bridget-bishop-biography-3530330

http://www.womenhistoryblog.com/2008/06/mary-towne-easty.html

https://historyofmassachusetts.org/mary-easty-salem/

https://www.thoughtco.com/mary-easty-biography-3530324

https://famous-trials.com/salem/2040-sal-beas

https://historyofmassachusetts.org/the-toothaker-family-witches-or-witch-killers/

https://www.thoughtco.com/bridget-bishop-biography-3530330

https://historyofmassachusetts.org/the-trial-of-rebecca-nurse/

https://famous-trials.com/salem/2052-asa-nur

https://famous-trials.com/salem/2039-sal-bgoo

http://www.newenglandhistoricalsociety.com/dirty-laundry-and-a-friend-save-philip-english-from-the-salem-witch-trials/

http://salem.lib.virginia.edu/people/english.html

https://famous-trials.com/salem/2044-englishp-m

https://www.thoughtco.com/john-alden-jr-biography-3528118

https://historyofmassachusetts.org/john-aldens-account-of-his-witch-trial-examination/

https://allthatsinteresting.com/giles-corey-martha-corey

https://www.thoughtco.com/giles-corey-biography-3530320

https://historyofmassachusetts.org/the-curse-of-giles-corey/

https://people.ucls.uchicago.edu/~snekros/Salem%20Journal/People/ElbertD.html

https://historyofmassachusetts.org/alice-parker-salem/

https://www.legendsofamerica.com/ma-witches-r-s/

https://historyofmassachusetts.org/samuel-wardwell-salem/

https://www.thoughtco.com/ann-pudeator-biography-3528112

http://www.womenhistoryblog.com/2008/07/margaret-stevenson-scott.html

http://www.womenhistoryblog.com/2008/06/mary-ayer-parker.html

http://salem.lib.virginia.edu/n68.html

https://www.u-s-history.com/pages/h2534.html

http://salem.lib.virginia.edu/people/i_mather.html

https://www.legendsofamerica.com/ma-witches-u-z/

https://www.thoughtco.com/salem-witch-trials-timeline-3530778

https://www.thoughtco.com/lydia-dustin-biography-3530331

https://www.legendsofamerica.com/ma-witches-d/

https://historyofmassachusetts.org/reverend-samuel-parris/

https://famous-trials.com/salem/2038-sal-bhat

https://www.thoughtco.com/elizabeth-proctor-about-3529972

http://thesalemwitchtrials0.weebly.com/the-hobbs-family.html

https://phaneuf.net/blog/funeral-traditions-in-colonial-new-england

http://www.newenglandhistoricalsociety.com/seven-strange-facts-colonial-funerals/

https://www.encyclopedia.com/people/history/us-history-biographies/horace-gray

http://mentalfloss.com/article/68420/what-animal-magnetism

https://erenow.net/common/america-bewitched/20.php

https://timespelunking.wordpress.com/2012/11/03/americas-last-withcraft-trial/

https://www.historyandheadlines.com/may-14-1878-last-american-witchcraft-trial-guessed-salem/

https://www.uh.edu/engines/epi1037.htm

https://history.howstuffworks.com/history-vs-myth/drugged-salem-witchtrial3.htm

Illustration I: https://commons.wikimedia.org/wiki/File:Matteson-witch.jpg

Illustration II: https://upload.wikimedia.org/wikipedia/commons/b/b1/SalemWitchcraftTrial_large.jpg

Illustration III:
https://commons.wikimedia.org/wiki/File:Giles_Corey_restored.jpg

Illustration IV:
https://commons.wikimedia.org/wiki/File:Salem_witch2_courtesy_copy.jpg

Illustration V:
https://commons.wikimedia.org/wiki/File:Salem_innocence.jpg

Made in the USA
Middletown, DE
14 December 2024

67020701R00071